RIGHT
LEADER

RIGHT
TIME

DISCOVER YOUR LEADERSHIP STYLE
FOR A WINNING CAREER AND COMPANY

RIGHT LEADER RIGHT TIME

ROBERT **JORDAN** & OLIVIA **WAGNER**

MEDIA

Published 2022 by Gildan Media LLC
aka G&D Media
www.GandDmedia.com

For more information about *Right Leader Right Time* and FABS Leadership, visit www .RightLeader.com where you can take the FABS Leadership Assessment. Contact the authors at info@RightLeader.com.

Front Cover design by Kostis Pavlou

Interior design by Meghan Day Healey of Story Horse, LLC

Library of Congress Cataloging-in-Publication Data is available upon request

ISBN: 978-1-7225-0567-7

10 9 8 7 6 5 4 3 2 1

Contents

Preface

When Sophie Jordan was fourteen days old, she weighed one pound and five ounces. About the same as four size D batteries. In the hush and beeps of a hospital neonatal intensive care unit, she lay in an incubator connected to intravenous lines and heart monitors. While she was breathing well thanks to a ventilator supplying air to her lungs, two of the major arteries to her heart had not separated at birth as they were meant to. She needed open-heart surgery.

My wife, Sharon, and I (Robert) were first-time parents, trying to understand how a newborn that looked more like a plucked chicken than a baby could survive surgery. We waited, and waited, pacing back and forth, not knowing what to expect. Praying for life to continue, hoping there *was* hope for our new daughter.

The door to the NICU opened and a woman walked in with a line of people trailing behind. She introduced herself, and without knowing why or how, I remember thinking in the instant before Dr. Marleta Reynolds spoke that we were in good hands. No, change that. I *knew* we were in great hands.

One moment I was so keyed up it was hard to breathe. Steel bands around my chest, tightening. Heart hammering like I was about to enter a cage fight to the death. And then Marleta Reynolds arrived and everything went quiet. It was not a conscious reaction, and I don't remember what she said. It didn't matter. I felt we were in the presence of something powerful, momentous, and positive. A professional so well trained, aware, accomplished, confident, and ready for the task at hand that worry was beside the point.

The right leader had shown up at just the right time.

Luckily, Sophie had a successful operation twenty-three years ago. Her care, and the feeling I got knowing she was in capable hands, sums up a lot of what I and my coauthor, Olivia Wagner, have seen in successful organizations.

When the right leader shows up, everyone breathes easy. Motivation and purposeful work spike, and people feel a sense of calm and direction knowing that good things are happening, great results will naturally occur, and there is movement toward a brighter future.

Introduction to FABS Leadership Styles

Think of a time you felt completely in your element leading an organization, team, or project. You were energized by the work and by the challenges in front of you. You knew you were the best person for the job and your results proved it.

Maybe you are in a role that gives you that feeling right now. Or you might feel a bit uneasy and have a hard time coming up with an answer. Maybe even envious of people who have been able to get in that zone or reach that high peak in their work. No matter what your reaction, if you desire to become a better leader, we tell you this: you are in the right place. We are going to help you discover how to magnify your strengths as a leader so you can be more effective in your career and the companies you lead.

Leadership is at the core of how organizations succeed or, more often than not, fail. So how is it that some leaders succeed brilliantly and repeatedly, while many others fail to deliver the goods? This question has been *the* driving force in our quest to work with and invest in only the best leaders and organizations, culminating in our research, interviews, and in the writing of this book.

A little bit of background about us, your coauthors, first. Robert Jordan launched his first company at the age of twenty-six, when he set out to create *Online Access*, the first magazine to cover the quickly evolving world of online services, computer bulletin boards, and the internet. It was a bumpy ride. Running out of cash. Sleepless nights. Going bust after just two years, then showing up in federal bankruptcy court to bid and buy back the assets to start again. The magazine ultimately skyrocketed onto the *Inc.* 500 list of fastest growing companies before it was sold to a big publishing company.

But even at the best part of that journey, he was a jack-of-all-trades, and it was frustrating being spread too thin. The experience did lead, however, to discovering the exact roles and responsibilities where he excelled, and more importantly—much more importantly—learning the value of partnering and coming to trust other leaders for their unique forms of genius. Following the sale of the magazine, Robert set out to help other owners and investors launch tech products and ultimately sell to strategic buyers.

In 2009 Robert teamed up with a new graduate from the University of Michigan, Olivia Wagner, to launch a worldwide network for what was then an underground community of interim and project-based executives. The concept of leadership-on-demand was new to Olivia, but what began as a job turned into a calling to help organizations tackle big challenges by matching them with great leadership resources. But how to ensure a successful match was made? We set out to discover the holy grail—the secret or elusive qualities, skills, mindset, and abilities that differentiate the ordinary from the extraordinary.

We had to know: What causes off-the-charts great performance, far above the average?

Identifying Inspiring Leadership

Our journey to identify the DNA of inspired and inspiring leadership took us on parallel tracks. We wrote and published *How They Did It: Billion Dollar Insights from the Heart of America*, a book of forty-five Q&A interviews with company founders who each launched from scratch, grew, and sold a company for $100 million or more, or IPO'd at $300 million or more.

In interviewing luminaries for *How They Did It* including Joe Mansueto, founder of Morningstar; Dick Costolo, CEO of Twitter; and Eric Lefkofsky, cofounder of Groupon, InnerWorkings, and Tempus, we learned that core to virtually every company founder's experience was a tale of surviving their company's near-death experiences.

At the same time, we continued to seek out and deploy rock star CEOs, CFOs, and other executives into companies around the globe. More than 5,600 executives showed up on our proverbial doorstep hailing from sixty-two countries and forty-six states from which a select few were deemed to be our incredibles, showing both the results and the chops to push reinvention, growth, turnaround, or change.

Screening out the mediocre from the rock stars is not as simple as looking at someone's track record. Mindset proved to be even more important. Sure, a résumé is telling of someone's capabilities, but it's static and like looking in a rearview mirror. We needed to determine how someone would jump into *action*—how they are wired for the challenge ahead.

Introducing the FABS Leadership Styles

Sit four friends down—an architect, a chef, a graphic designer, and a financial analyst—around a table on launch day of the hottest new restaurant in town and ask them what they think. Chances are, here's what you'll hear:

- The architect might comment on the structure of the building, its space, how the light streams in, and the look and feel of how its configuration serves and welcomes you.
- The chef might focus on the presentation of the meal while identifying the unique flavors and spices at play.
- The graphic designer may first notice the menu and design elements around the room.
- The financial analyst could visualize how much investment went into the restaurant and what kinds of returns success means for the investors.

Your frame of reference colors your perceptions. Likewise, accomplished leaders have a frame of reference that results in a strong suit—an elemental quality or leadership mode—that defines their highest and best use.

In our quest to define what separates successful leaders from the rest, we identified four modes or styles of leadership, each with a unique mindset, skill set, process, approach, system of operation, and drive: Fixer, Artist, Builder, and Strategist (FABS for short). The match between an organization given its particular needs, stage, and size, and a leader operating in their favored FABS mode is vital in understanding how some leaders produce genius results time after time, while others suffer in frustration and defeat.

THE FOUR FABS LEADERSHIP STYLES

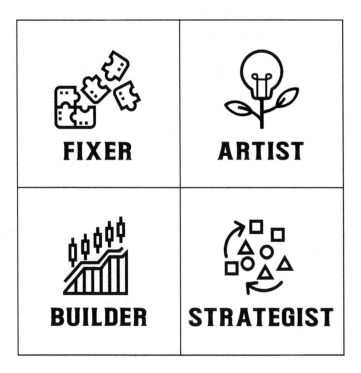

THE FIXER

This leader sees what's broken and one or more ways to fix it. Fixers are drawn to even the most dysfunctional or toxic situations. They bring order out of chaos, cut through messes, conserve cash and resources, and figure out what needs to be expanded, cut, streamlined, aligned, and organized to create something better. Send a Fixer into a company that is hemorrhaging, and they know how to stop the bleeding. The worse the circumstances, seemingly the better for the expert Fixer. It's not that this leader lacks sympathy or caring for the team. Far from it. It's the innate desire to seek maximum challenge, taking on firefighting that other leaders would run from. Once the fix is complete, it's a dopamine rush only satisfied by the next crisis.

THE ARTIST

This leader starts with a blank canvas and creates a work of art, whether product, service, technology, message, campaign, platform, company, organization, or movement. Artist leaders envision the finished work and are able to enlist, enroll, sell, and revolutionize. They trust their ingenuity, resourcefulness, and out-of-the-box ability to innovate and move a team or organization past lethargy or stagnation. These are the leaders driving revolutionary change, creating the new and different, whether at a product, company, country, or world level. It can be a long road for the Artist whose seemingly crazy ideas may be met with laughter, until a moment comes when the movement engulfs the late adopters and they finally say, "Oh, now I get it." And then the Artist is no longer the mad scientist.

THE BUILDER

This leader makes foundation and structure for an organization to enter new markets and thrive. Helping ramp up a company, product, or division from small—even a handful of employees—to multimillion- or multibillion-dollar success takes a level of scrappiness and vision for what the fully constructed end-product looks like. The Builder loves growth mode, where expansion into new markets and increases far beyond market averages is the goal. They have an innate ability to build teams and create systems and processes from scratch. A master Builder is a huge asset to organizations that need help getting past a ceiling in their growth, but they may not necessarily stick around when markets and systems become mature and established. Once size, maturity, and complexity of the organization has moved beyond a personal span of control, Builders tend to hand off to explore the next market opportunity.

THE STRATEGIST

This leader operates at scale, leading an organization with a diverse agenda, navigating complexity where direction is far beyond their personal span of control. Strategists enhance structure, fortifying repeatable, defensible systems with long-term competitive advantages. Steady and detailed in approach, they provide strategy that an organization—whether a team of 1,000 or 100,000—can be held accountable to. With a focus on metrics, Strategists serve as voice and conductor for short- and long-term vision that managers, teams, and divisions will turn into tactical plans and execution throughout the organization. Deploying, developing, and conducting the many pieces at play, the Strategist ensures that there is always forward movement, knowing that even established market leaders can be ripe for disruption.

Likely you already see yourself in one or more of these styles. You'll have ample opportunities to identify ways to up your leadership game as you read into the lives and leadership stories of the Fixers, Artists, Builders, and Strategists in the following chapters.

The labels Fixer, Artist, Builder, and Strategist may sound obvious, but when you dive deeper into each style, it's amazing how distinct they are. The differences among successful styles are so wide you could drive a truck through them. What is fertile ground for one leader would be a disaster for another. Different stages in an organization's evolution call for unique leadership styles and capabilities. Match the right leader in the right mode with the right organization, and magic can happen.

To more rigorously begin to prove or disprove these four modes, we interviewed seventy-five successful leaders, some well known and others who flew under the radar, including a handful of psychologists and experts on leadership, as a sanity check.

A pattern emerged. As we explored leadership approaches and track records, we also looked at the choices that each leader made in determining their best career track. The results were telling. Time and again, we saw that success was never one size fits all.

No one, no matter how talented, was best in all situations. The most effective leaders did not try to be all things to all people. They knew their strengths.

Your Highest and Best Use

We consumers demand specialization and deep expertise in most aspects of modern life. In the legal profession there are at least twenty separate disciplines, for example, from bankruptcy to corporate to criminal law, entertainment, labor, tax, personal injury, and intellectual property. Each its own specialty, requiring the best in each field to keep learning, practicing, improving—lifelong.

In healthcare there are 120 specialties, from anesthesiology, cardiology, and dermatology to immunology, oncology, neurology, pediatrics, and urology. The benefits of such specialization over the past seventy-five years are so vast as to be astounding, from better health to relief from pain and suffering to dramatically increased longevity.

We are now in such a beneficial place that you would no more expect your obstetrician to operate on your heart than a criminal defense attorney to file patents for you.

Why then, in the management of organizations, is the exact role and application of a leader still so ill-defined?

We applaud the *appearance* of an all-encompassing skill as, well, all-encompassing. But it is not the same as highest and best use, or the feeling we get when we're operating in a role that leads to feelings of endless expansion, fascination, learning, flow, accomplishment, capability, and never-ending improvement.

Power comes from recognizing, accepting, and acting whole-heartedly in alignment with your unique wiring. This alignment, however, need not be selfish in the sense of accounting only for your-self. Effective leaders tap into their best abilities and operate in their most authentic expression of their own style of leading, while show-ing qualities of loyalty, mentoring, and sacrifice. This excellence is a force multiplier everywhere from the boardroom to the shop floor; from the surgical operating suite to the halls of Congress; from a soc-cer field to a social network.

Rejecting One Size Fits All

We observe time and again executives firing on all cylinders, diving into a dominant FABS leadership style, not hunting around the dial searching for anything other than their intrinsic self. The opposite are those who spread themselves thin, force-fitting into all kinds of situations, personas, and roles.

For the ambitious, the temptation is real. The more accomplished we become, the more we can and should stretch. All well and good. But saying yes to any opportunity that comes our way, trying to expand in all directions, all competencies, and performing equally well no matter what? That tactic only works until it breaks.

"We can customize our behaviors, but it's a catch-22," says leader-ship expert and organizational psychologist John Behr. "We want to be realistic and learn to give and take in our organizations or in our life, but not give or take in a way that's not at least fairly close to an authentic expression of ourselves. Otherwise it's not sustainable."

With some rare exceptions. Winston Churchill was a master Fixer, Strategist, and Artist. His speeches and broadcasts at the onset of World War II proved him as a word painter of the first order, not only keeping up Britain's resolve, but convincing a withdrawn, isolationist United States to enter the war. Sheer artistry in language. Churchill's canvas was the Western world.

Great leaders are rich with abilities brought to bear as the situation demands and with seeming excellence and authenticity no matter the challenge. Nonetheless, we suggest leaders have a dominant, go-to mode that becomes richer, more powerful, and valued over time and across accumulated experience. Voters threw Churchill out of office immediately on the triumphant close of World War II. The Fixer was out. They were sick of war.

No leader is perfect in all situations.

In our work screening executives, we often see leaders who should be at the most powerful point in their career, instead flailing around, saying they can do it all, when in reality their focus is not focus, but rather a diluted hodgepodge of skills and desires, preventing them from real clarity and an ability to reject what is not a fit.

When we are honest with ourselves, it is easier to acknowledge that while we can, in fact, weave in and out of different roles as an organization grows, pivots, and hits inevitable bumps, we don't enjoy all modes equally well; and more to the point, we don't excel equally.

Testifying at a trial in July 2021 to defend his decision to combine Tesla and Solar City, Elon Musk was asked about running the company day-to-day. "I rather hate it and I would much prefer to spend my time on design and engineering, which is what intrinsically I like doing," he responded.

He sums up in one sentence what we have found is the key mindset that over 50 percent of all leaders get wrong over the course of their careers. Musk was candid in both what he hated, and what he knew of his intrinsic nature—what he was drawn to like iron filings to a magnet. He knew himself.

Most importantly, it's the stakeholders around us who can see the variability of results and know, sometimes better than we do, where we shine brightest and where we tend to fade.

"If the leader is poorly aligned with the situation, that is going to be a problem from day one until the end," says Fixer and business saver David Johnson. "I think it's incumbent on every leader when they look at a situation to not only be able to advocate for themselves and say 'Yes, this is exactly what I do, I'm the best person for you,' but also to say, 'This is too far afield for me. This is not the thing that I am best at.'"

Cutting Off Options

Successful people make career decisions that cut off options. The word *decide* comes from the Latin for "to cut off." You might feel that your first job was an accident or stroke of luck, but when you look back on a successful career, choices over time become more intentional. It's as if a magnetic attraction was pulling at you, to encourage, nurture, and advance one path over another, one type of work, role, or place over all others.

Troy Henikoff is a seasoned company Builder who cofounded SurePayroll, the first internet payroll service in the US. While Henikoff loved the early days of launching and growing SurePayroll, as the company got larger and larger, both he and his board realized he was a much better founder than CEO. It took a lot of soul searching, but he recognized that moving on to his next endeavor was best for him and for the future of the business.

"If I know I've got to do a task to get to see the business successful, I will do it," Henikoff says, "but I woke up one day realizing that we had eighty employees and I was spending all my time managing managers. I much preferred rolling up my sleeves and getting dirt under my fingernails working with customers and creating products than being a CEO." Good move. The company was acquired by Paychex in 2011.

Now if at this point you're thinking, Oh, I get it, they're saying I've gotta stay in my lane? the answer is no. *You* determine your lane, your route, your life trip, and it could have lots of detours or dead ends. But at some point, success demands you find your on-ramp, your personal freeway, maybe an Autobahn with no speed limit whatsoever.

We also aren't saying that you should end up performing like everyone else. Far from it. Four types of nucleotides make up the DNA of all biological forms: adenine, thymine, cytosine, and guanine. Whether it's your aunt Margaret, your pet poodle, or an oak tree, just these four nucleotides repeat in combination billions of times to produce all flora and fauna in every wildest variation. The four FABS modes typify every leader, but to infinite degrees of variation.

Underlying all of this is the feeling of being enough, of becoming confident in your style of leadership, to know the areas you are drawn to and the areas that do not serve you. That is enough. It is not settling for less, or rationalizing. But it is a determination to not be all things to all people.

How to Use This Book

If you can recognize the right opportunities for you, and the right moments to bring in complementary skill sets around you—or exit to the next project, team, client, venue, or venture—our bet is that you will find more success, more fulfillment, and more love of the game. We know, it's easier said than done. Read on. You're going to hear from a wide variety of leaders how they did it. Leaders forge a path, no matter what, and seek opportunities that play to their best mode, and reject what does not feel like their highest and best use.

Right Leader Right Time breaks into four major chapters, one each for Fixer, Artist, Builder, and Strategist. Within these chapters are sections including an in-depth profile on one leader operating in that style, an overview of traits, and finally a look at leaders in action and the unique habits and approach each style exemplifies. In chapter 5, we consider the three core principles that are the foundation for all FABS leadership style success and how they could apply in your organization.

Some of the examples in the pages that follow may sound superhuman or just ridiculously successful, yet no one started that way. We spoke with a mix of executives in the C-suite, midlevel managers, and small business owners. Working to become a better leader applies whether you direct the efforts of 10,000 or just one other person, and whether you are driving for leadership of a big team or are determined to stay lean and nimble and outsource as much as possible.

Our goal is to provide insights into your own best and highest work, igniting a spark—a nudge—toward bigger and better opportunities and more significance in the organizations you work with and care about. We hope you feel even more empowered to leave your positive stamp on the world. To reinforce your path to peace of mind and fulfilling your soul's desire.

If you want to discover more about your specific mode of leadership, you can visit RightLeader.com and take the FABS Leadership Assessment. We also pose questions for you in the chapters that follow to help you explore and determine your primary leadership style.

1.
THE FIXER

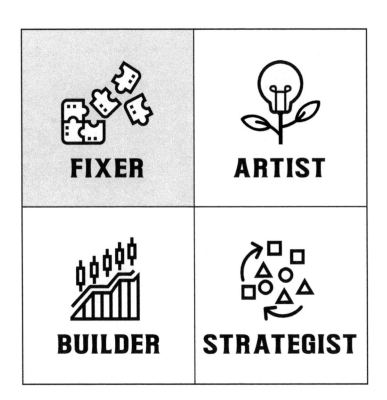

FIXER

ARTIST

BUILDER

STRATEGIST

A Fixer Story:
Making the Impossible Save

Though only an eight-hour drive from Bucharest to Arad, Romania, it felt like ages to Eric Kish who was now sitting face-to-face with the Bulibasha—the King of the Roma (informally known as the Gypsies). Adrenaline was pumping as he began the negotiation of a lifetime for the only thing that could save his now dying company. The Bulibasha held all the cards, and Kish knew this would determine the fate of his company—and career.

Kish had taken over an oil refinery just weeks before, a hulking complex of buildings and machinery in Bucharest, Romania. Formerly the crown jewel of the communist country's efforts to produce its own gasoline and petrochemicals, the state-owned refinery called Petromidia was acquired out of bankruptcy for $7 million cash by a private investor group, and it was Kish's job to do the impossible: save it.

The company had been run as a virtual dictatorship for the previous forty years. It was a culture where, Kish says, "You did not open your mouth unless you were given permission." There was a half billion dollars in overdue debt, negative equity, and the livelihood of 3,600 people was now in his hands. The devastation of September 11 subsequently hit, and all refining margins plummeted, so that for every ton of oil they processed, they lost money.

Most people would run as fast as they could in the opposite direction. Kish jumped at the opportunity. "I'm restless," he says. "Show me a challenge, I sleep on it for a night, and next day I'm like, screw it, let's do it." It was that attitude that got him into the turnaround business to begin with. When an investor approached Kish saying he wanted to buy and turnaround *all* the bankrupt refineries in Eastern Europe, Kish didn't think twice. "I just said, 'Absolutely, I'm in.'"

Soon after he took control of Petromidia, the situation got worse. Permits to run the refinery were expiring in two months, causing the plant to shut down. Even after getting the plant back up and running a few months later, bigger problems loomed.

"Boss, we have a problem," came the voice over the telephone on a Saturday morning. A twenty-story-tall filtering tower, which was vital for turning crude oil into gasoline, had exploded under water pressure testing and was now nothing but a heap of scrap metal, destroyed beyond repair. No tower, no plant. No plant, no oil.

It seemed to be the final nail in the coffin. A new tower would take twelve months to manufacture and maybe another four months to install. They couldn't survive a year and a half, let alone just a few months.

Kish recalled his time serving in the IDF, the Israel Defense Forces, where he learned to develop what he believes is his strongest leadership trait: adaptability. "You train for perfection, but you expect the plan to go wrong immediately," Kish says. "When things are moving so fast you get disrupted out of the blue, the only thing that will keep you alive is adapting to your situation and your actions to whatever is happening around you."

It was this training that gave Kish the tools to start changing the culture, to prepare the organization to face the unexpected. By empowering his team to think and act on their own, he knew they stood a chance of digging their way out of the chaos. After the tower explosion, he launched meetings to brainstorm the craziest ideas they could dream up. His goal was to tap the brainpower of everyone and anyone at the refinery. Whether by method or luck, hope arrived from the maintenance department.

The maintenance engineer ducked his head into Kish's office saying he had an idea. He had learned that an old refinery was being cut up at a scrapyard owned by the Roma, a tribe of nomadic people in Eastern Europe who also happened to control the scrap metal trade. Might they have a filter tower still intact? Just days later Kish found himself in Arad, Romania, at the grand house of the Bulibasha—the King of the Roma.

The Roma arrived in Europe a thousand years ago with traditions dating even further back. You cannot get married without the approval of the Bulibasha, and any talk of business could not happen without time to eat, drink, and socialize. There were twenty Roma in the room, and though Kish felt the ticking down of the hours working against him, he knew they would not trust him unless he respected their customs. Dinner spanned five hours, but as luck would have it, Kish was able to trade many stories about his father who was born just 100 kilometers north of Arad on the Hungarian border.

On the second day, business could be discussed after a heavy breakfast that started with a Transylvanian specialty, palinka. The Roma pride themselves on the strength of this alcoholic drink, but to keep a clear head and not offend his host, Kish pretended to sip the boozy breakfast.

Finally, the Bulibasha put his cards on the table. He wanted $200,000 for the massive tower of shiny metal he had in his possession. Kish knew that a new tower would come with a hefty $2 million to $3 million price tag, so it was a good opening offer. He also knew that the region operated by what they called the Turkish style of negotiation, meaning you bargain for everything. The offer was just an opening price, and if he showed the slightest hint of relief or acceptance, he was dead in the water.

"Forget it, I'm leaving," he said, as he got up and moved to the door.

The Bulibasha rose as well, saying "No, sir, I see you are a serious businessman. What if I give you two towers for $200,000?"

It was everything Kish could do to not react. With a blank expression, he turned around and asked, "What do you mean two towers?" The Bulibasha explained that they had two identical towers that he could offer up to Kish for the right price. This would completely change the picture for the refinery. With two towers they could increase capacity fourfold to extract sulfur out of gasoline. It would be a huge step forward.

The game continued over three days of negotiation, leading to the purchase of two towers and creating a completely new and bright future for Petromidia.

After restructuring the mountain of debt and increasing automation, operating efficiencies rose and sales came in at $1.2 billion. Production costs had come down 65 percent while revenue and production more than tripled. In just three years, the company had massively turned around and was ready for its public debut. In 2004 they IPO'd at a valuation of $450 million, an eye-popping return on the initial $7 million investment.

Most telling of a great Fixer is how they approach the team, especially during periods of uncertainty or distress. Many so-called expert turnaround executives have only one playbook: slash and burn, cut as many heads as possible. At Petromidia 3,600 lives hung in the balance, an employee count way in excess of the needs of a modern refinery, which seldom requires more than 400 workers to run well.

Kish assigned 550 employees to the refinery, and then came an act of brilliance on the part of the team. They split up the company into eight separately branded operating entities. Each had its own mission, which was first and foremost to support the group. But each entity now had a second mandate: to face outward to the market, providing their own services and generating customers independently. He set a goal that within five years each one of the new companies had to generate 50 percent or more of their revenues outside the group by mastering a market, whether it was distribution of oil or retail sales. The strategy worked so well that everyone who wanted to stay, could stay.

Kish didn't stop there. Six additional acquisitions and turnarounds followed to create the largest oil company in southeastern Europe, eventually acquired in 2008 for $3.8 billion.

EARNING ATTENTION, FAST

A Fixer at heart, Eric Kish is energized at first sight of a troubled situation. He is now working on his twelfth turnaround. The bigger the challenge, the better.

The Fixer enters when a company's cash flow tanks, fraud is suspected, morale is in the toilet, the board is fighting, or market forces cause a crash in demand for goods or services. Fixing doesn't mean pointing fingers, barking orders, or chopping heads. True Fixers have refined their ability to listen carefully, to assemble a winning team, to collaborate and diagnose the root of the problem, to put controls in place, and to mentor the team that will sustain long-term company health.

After the success of Petromidia, Kish told the *Wall Street Journal*, "Don't bother speaking to me about pressure, temperature or any technical data. Speak to me about dollars; that's the language I understand."

When an organization is running out of money, or if the end of the runway from investors is looming, Kish argues it's actually easier to manage a turnaround. When the Fixer shows up, everyone knows that much of what was taken for granted will change, so you don't really have to explain to people that change is coming. You have their attention.

"It's like you have cancer and you're trying an experiment that was never done, because what could be worse?" he says. "You have a free hand at experimenting that, in normal circumstances, a board would probably say no."

It's that makeup that attracts Kish to distressed and dire situations. "Look, stress is everywhere," he told us when we interviewed him for this book. "The question is how you manage it. In the midst of crisis, when everything falls apart around you, the most important thing is to remain calm. Don't rush into things. Have confidence."

You could say Eric Kish's upbringing was a proving ground or foreshadowing for his chosen career. Growing up in communist Romania, he thought he was doomed to work in a government-assigned job. He'd already had a stint in compulsory military service in the Romanian Army, which he describes as "stupid beyond belief." He couldn't stand the thought of a forced career at low wages, so while studying electrical engineering at the national university, he sang and played lead guitar at weddings for cash under the table. He thought life as a musician might be the career for him until the day he got an unexpected call from his father.

"Son, I'm not coming back," his dad told him. His father, who traveled a lot for the government had decided to defect to the United States, which meant Eric and his family would be declared the family of a traitor.

"You live in government housing. You go to a university which is paid by the government. You don't own anything. It's free, but the government kicked us out of our home and me out of university because we didn't deserve it anymore," Eric recalls. He was twenty-two and now the man of the house with an eleven-year-old sister and a mother who was struggling with bipolar disorder. It was a heavy weight to bear. With nowhere to live and no income, he had to scramble to figure out a way for them to survive.

Kish grew up reading about Israel and knew of his mother's Jewish heritage but could never move there because it would be the end of his father's career. Now that his father was safe in the US, all bets were off. He showed up at the Israeli Embassy asking if they had a way to get him out. They said to hang on for four months and, in the meantime, show up at the Israeli Embassy every two weeks for a cash stipend as a means to survive.

"Those were dark times," Kish says, describing having to jump from house to house with his mother and little sister, staying with different friends who were kind enough to keep him and his family in their basements.

Despite the hardships, Kish says leaving Romania was probably the best decision his father made in his life for his family. Four months following his father's defection, Eric Kish, his mom, and sister emigrated to Israel, and Eric—out of gratitude and loyalty—joined the IDF, where he was thrown into another form of chaos: the threat of war.

"In Israel you train like war is tomorrow," he says. Any morning you could wake up to a completely new landscape. Kish credits his training in the IDF for lessons he applies to business today. "You have to have situational awareness to collect information fast—faster than your enemies—and provide it real-time at the point of decision," he says. "If the plan doesn't work, throw it out the door and come up with something else."

Kish points to what Israelis call front-line decision-making, trusting low-level leaders to do the right thing. In his role as CEO, he explains that he doesn't have to do everything, but seeks to create the context for those projects and tasks to happen and "trust that my people are well trained and smart enough to make their own decisions, create their own plans, and execute on them."

Kish doesn't talk much at the beginning of a new leadership role. He listens and does everything he can to show people that he cares. He has to build trust. "Most of the people I encounter in turnarounds want it to be successful and want to be part of it," he says. "The commitment levels that I find are extraordinary, and the moment a trusting relationship begins, then the journey is phenomenal."

It's this open-mindedness that brings problems to the surface. Every problem is meant to be examined, not to place blame. Find what works, what doesn't, and how it can be improved. Doing this from a positive framework, the team can go from downtrodden to openly evaluating every aspect and situation. When new problems arise, Kish brings everyone in a room to brainstorm and find the best solution.

NO MORE BEST PRACTICES

"We kill what is called 'best practices,'" Kish says. "Best practices that work for one company might be the worst practice for another." He points to the management fad of the 1980s, when the book *In Search of Excellence* popularized the idea that top companies operate on the same set of best practices. Laughing, he says that just a few years after publication half of the companies on the list would not make the list anymore.

Fixers are attuned to changing environments. When he parachutes into a company, Kish uses the phrase "practices that work for us" with a caveat that a practice that works for them today might not work tomorrow. He advocates for continual refining of what works and what doesn't. During their brainstorming sessions, the team always has the option to kill a practice and invent something new to move forward faster.

"When new habits form within the company, that's the measure of winning for me," Kish says. His main focus is on changing behavior, or what he believes are big-picture changes that can alter the organization's course dramatically. He concentrates on remaining calm to guide the team through chaos, leveraging its talent and technical knowledge.

His go-to morning ritual is the Daily Standup, where the team meets (virtually and in person), quickly tell what they did yesterday, what they're going to do today, and if they have any hurdles. Kish says, "It becomes a habit when people automatically resort to that in order to get situationally aware." When the team was trying to push a new product and decided their cadence was too slow, they increased the Daily Standup to three times a day to get fast-moving software projects done on time and on budget.

He acknowledges he's not good at everything and credits his strength as a leader to the muscle-memory developed over twenty years in solving challenges: "I was very impulsive. I would fight for everything. I wouldn't let anyone else talk much because I knew exactly what needed to be done, and it needed to be done today." He says he operates differently now. "I am missing so much if I do that. Now, I listen to people, enable their ideas, and back them up with force to move *their* ideas forward. It is far more profitable than just pushing my ideas because I'm the boss."

Once the organization is back on firm ground, Kish brings in a new leader. His style, like most Fixers, can't help but look for the next mess to clean up. He describes it this way: "If you can put up with stress, with the ambiguity, and with the fact that you're always close to disaster . . . if you can navigate that, then the results can be exceptionally good."

The Fixer Leadership Mode

Successful leaders adopt a style—a mode of operation—as they grow. It can become as distinct as a fingerprint. For Fixers, style is the urge to make things right despite the magnitude of the crisis. Right now. Maybe markets crashed, or some other truly external cause can be cited, but in most cases something else is going on that leads to a Fixer being called in. Within established, entrenched organizations those problems run from corporate malfeasance, to financial losses, to botched boards, transactions, or operations. Not much fazes the Fixer.

Successful Fixers can be high profile or nearly anonymous. The saviors of Tyco, Twinkies, and Krispy Kreme are not household names, but their work has made high stress look easy from the outside. And of course, it's not always about the corporate world. Peter Ueberroth is widely credited with reversing the course of the modern Olympics, which had always been a sinkhole for billions of dollars in financial losses for the cities and countries hosting the games.

Ueberroth led the 1984 Summer Olympics in Los Angeles, shaking up the model and revamping everything from the sponsorship program to how broadcasting rights were structured. The first Olympics to be privately financed and managed, the venture yielded a surplus of $230 million, much of which was used to create a foundation to support youth sports throughout Southern California.

THE NEED FOR SPEED

Velocity is mantra for the Fixer.

Peter Murphy, a veteran CEO who spent his career turning around private equity–backed companies, knows this well. "Velocity is the keyword for me," he says. "I keep thinking about it. I talk about it a lot. We've got to increase the velocity in approaching these issues, fixing these processes, developing new customers."

Speed is key. In the span of just forty-two months Murphy led and improved operations in seven different companies from nuclear radiation detection to automotive electronics to gaming. More than any other situation, crisis needs speed of change.

Lee Iacocca was a classic Fixer. Well known as the father of the Ford Mustang, he really kicked in gear on entry as CEO of Chrysler, which reported a massive $155 million loss on his first day on the job. He fired thirty-three of his thirty-five VPs, replaced ad agencies, persuaded union leaders to accept layoffs and pay cuts, and recruited new executives.

Without blinking he pushed the US Treasury to a controversial decision to bail out Chrysler. His example perfectly highlights the Fixer's ability to act at speed, be decisive, and do whatever is necessary to save the day. In 1984, a year after paying back the government, the company hit $2.4 billion in record high profits.

Histories of Napoleon Bonaparte and Alexander the Great each report how much their enemies respected and feared their speed in battle. These generals could maneuver masses of troops with lightning speed, outflanking their enemies before opposing forces knew what was happening.

Time is always of the essence for Fixers. Everyone claims they want to be nimble, but Fixers really mean it. In a crisis, the fires are real. Organizations feel as if the oxygen is being sucked out of the room. Cash is evaporating, people are leaving, customers have fled, the sheriff is at the door. Peter Murphy says: "Time is always the enemy. Time is always working against us because the longer it takes us to address issues, the more opportunity is lost."

Fixers are drawn to this extreme challenge in the form of crisis— the supreme point of need in an organization. The Fixer has time and controls on the brain, evaluating the most critical items such as cash burn, declining morale, and how to stabilize critical needs immediately.

"The first month or two, when it's really heavy-duty discovery, is what I enjoy most," explains Michelle Barnes who has turned around many nonprofit organizations, ranging from the Tourette Association of America to the largest food bank in Colorado. "You're looking for themes and threads. I don't have time to do a hundred things. I've got to pick three to five things to do really well. Picking those three or five things is everything. If you pick the wrong ones, the organization's not going to get healthier."

Chief Restructuring Officer David Johnson describes the vast information load that a Fixer is adept at navigating through: "All of a sudden everything is on the table—the leadership, the strategy, the product mix." With change being a driving force, Fixers have to hit the ground running and know how to prioritize.

Chief Executive John Short refers to himself as the company doctor, saying that he is typically called in by the board or someone on the management team to heal the situation when crisis hits. He recalls being asked to serve on the board of Joe Boxer, which at the time was facing default on its bank loans. "There were issues on the board, with the bank, the supply chain and with attorneys who wanted to throw the company into Chapter 11," Short says.

At the first board meeting, everyone argued that Chapter 11 (bankruptcy) was the only way out. Short convinced them to hold off, seeing that distribution channels were their biggest (solvable) problem. He immediately negotiated with the bank to give them another ninety days. He was appointed to CEO, and within a minuscule window of time, he worked his magic, expanding the product offering from high end to mass market. He licensed the brand to Kmart, which paid $50 million up front, giving him the ability to pay back the bank and get money returned to shareholders.

FOR LOVE OF URGENCY AND ADRENALINE

Fixers love intensity. They love the urgency and needs of the moment. Once that first adrenaline rush hits, and the satisfaction of successfully turning around an organization sets in, it's hard to turn down the next challenge.

So when John Short got a call from Sunglass Hut asking him to join the team, he couldn't resist. The company was a mess. Being a public company didn't help, as the SEC had gotten involved due to claims of faulty accounting. They had also acquired seven companies but hadn't properly integrated or accounted for them. If that wasn't enough, the board was in turmoil, with new board members coming in and experienced ones dropping off.

Short spent the next nine months cleaning up the international business, which spanned fifteen countries. Next in line to fix was the US, where he led 1,800 stores, restructuring the company and expanding the product line. The company reached profitability in eighteen months and later sold to Luxottica.

A crisis invariably means that the incumbent leadership has failed or was overcome by circumstances. In a time of intense difficulty and trouble, poor morale within an organization is the norm, and it can seem like there is no way out, no path to a brighter future. Eric Kish notes that in some ways crisis presents an easier leadership situation because it's more obvious what the leader has to do, and thus achieving buy-in from all stakeholders—employees, customers, vendors, owners, partners, community—can be much faster.

"Fixers not only run toward the burning building," says David Johnson, "but they must be able to inspire and motivate others to follow them in."

Peter Murphy points out one of the most critical differences between Fixers and other leaders: "When you're doing a turnaround, you're typically not trying to build a lot of structure, but you are trying to implement control. You're trying to put controls into your processes, controls into your financial systems."

Fixers have strong financial acumen and an analytic mindset, and yet many come to see their greatest achievements in working with the people around them. "I focus on the narrative. Finance is my specialty, but people react very strongly to a story. It is easy to lose people with just numbers," says David Johnson.

"I can go in as a Fixer, but the day I leave, if I haven't made everybody else part of the solution, the forward progress is going to stop," Michelle Barnes says, pointing to the need to empower the managers and rank and file within the organization. "I've got to have people who are willing to speak truth and offer better ideas. This means the organization will grow more organically."

Fixers seek internal resources to leverage that brainpower, create forward movement, and leave the legacy of past blunders behind. "In short order you have an opportunity to mentor half a dozen or more people and coach an even larger number as you upgrade the leadership team, as you give battlefield promotions to people who were buried under bad managers," David Johnson says.

If velocity is one side of the coin for a Fixer, the other side must surely read: calm. Despite the storm, to be excellent in crisis requires the calm born of past crises solved. The confidence to know—we can handle this. We've got this. In all of our interviews, we never heard a Fixer use the word *hurry*, despite how obvious the needs must be.

PRACTICALITY FIRST AND FOREMOST

Like many of the best Fixers, Dick Lindenmuth always showed a level of practicality that ingrained in him the view that many of the answers are already in the organization but had not been tapped. "I'm very much attracted to problem solving not because I'm brilliant, but because I like working with people and trying to find out what they think and making them successful," says Lindenmuth, who reset struggling businesses for thirty-plus years. [He recently passed away and left this wisdom for us all.]. "While I might do something differently than somebody else, any good systematic approach can work if it's supported, resources are there, and the priorities are established. If the problems and approach are described and agreed upon, almost anything can be solved."

Fixers tend to be straight shooters. Tell it like it is. In times of disaster, tough decisions are required, and leaders usually find that brutal honesty is necessary to move the needle. "There's no reason to not deliver full information around bad news or that somebody has an unfavorable review. Their performance didn't meet expectations. Nobody benefits by getting a free pass," says Mike Bartikoski, who has spent his career fixing broken supply chains and operations in companies from Hershey and Pepsi to Nestlé and Coca-Cola.

Many successful leaders—about 50 percent of the people we've interviewed over the years and for this book—intuitively identify themselves as Fixers. It makes sense. One of the most prominent determinants of a successful leader is how they perform under stress and how they solve problems in times of trouble. The challenge could be anything from team to management, to finances or markets, sales or operations. No matter what the case, it's anything but business as usual. There was a problem to be solved, and the accountable leader must run into the fire, no matter the cost.

All great leaders run the Fixer gauntlet sooner or later even if it's not their strongest form of leadership expression. Steve Jobs is remembered for Apple's brilliant innovation, only made possible by first saving the company when it was ninety days away from bankruptcy.

When COVID-19 hit, decimating travel and tourism, Airbnb could have become a statistic. Instead, the company took fast action, including a revamp in favor of local listings over long distance travels. CEO Brian Chesky was reported saying, "I did not know that I would make ten years' worth of decisions in ten weeks."

Tom Britton, CEO of Gateway Foundation, the largest nonprofit addiction treatment center services in the US, described how without warning, Google cut them off and refused to allow them to advertise online. The company immediately spun into crisis mode. "That was a big channel of business for us. It was our entire margin for the year," he says, recalling that he asked himself, What am I going to do? I can't force Google to do what I want. Britton and his team went into overdrive, coming up with new ways to promote their services and ultimately fundamentally restructuring their marketing approach.

All successful organizations experience points of maximum stress that test a leader's abilities. We, however, single out the dominant mode of Fixer as someone who has a repeat propensity and excellence in fixing broken situations, distress, and disaster—time after time. A Fixer gravitates toward the overwhelming and seemingly impossible challenge and relishes in the experience—good or bad—enough to do it all over again. And again. And again.

In the movie *Apocalypse Now*, Martin Sheen plays an army captain stuck in a Saigon hotel awaiting new orders. He is far from relieved to be away from the terror of combat in the Vietnamese jungle and instead finds himself worried he's going soft. He is champing at the bit to get back into battle. The Fixer needs the fix.

KEEPING IT LINEAR

Beyond the battle, the Fixer also is drawn to linearity and sequence, typically working on one broken, bleeding, or troubled entity at a time. It's focusing 24/7 on all-consuming work. Fix it—whether it takes six months or six years—and then move on to the next. The pattern is triage, plan, repair, fix, move on, and repeat.

"Fixers get bored," organizational psychologist John Behr describes. "The modern age of compartmentalized leadership and increasingly project-based roles plays perfectly for the Fixer leader." Their success is to work themselves out of the job.

It doesn't mean everything always goes perfectly. Some situations are beyond repair, and the Fixer ends up disposing of assets, closing the doors, and turning out the lights. So long as the Fixer has a positive track record overall, they'll stay at it, from save to save.

This points to what brings Fixer leaders to their next turnaround role. "Fixers like drama, but they're not sadists," says Dr. Behr. "They don't want to necessarily punish people, but they do like to effect change in a way they can see. For a Fixer in an organization with some equilibrium, the drama is gone. They don't usually want to be there anymore." That means the Fixer leader has to move on.

IF IT AIN'T BROKE, BREAK IT

What if a Fixer sticks around too long or is put in a stable situation? Surprisingly, most Fixers do not take offense to Jim Dolan's sentiment, "If I put a Fixer into one of my companies and it's not broken, he'll break it. Just so he can fix it." Their reaction is, "Yeah, so?"

"There's a risk that you would break it because you get your endorphins from fixing things, but I also like to think you can use that need to fix things for good and actually make things better," CEO Michelle Barnes says. "I like fixing things, but sometimes you're seeking more upside. That next big bold move might be fixing the infrastructure or changing the culture or going into a new line of business."

Even stable organizations may need some form of shake-up and rejiggering from a fresh, outside perspective. Peter Murphy thinks that's just being proactive. "While a company could appear to be doing well, they might be driving toward a cliff, and so a successful company often takes a turnaround as well," he says. "You're turning people around, and you're turning programs, projects, processes around because there's always ample room to fix things."

Jim Dolan made seventy-six acquisitions during his tenure at publishing company Dolan Media where he realized, "The Fixer approach is reasonable every time we made an acquisition." Even if acquisitions were not fixer-uppers, his approach would be to ask lots of open-ended questions, leaving all judgment aside.

"No matter how good your research before you buy, you always learn more after you own the place," he says, explaining that their questions led to a series of instructions to stop close to a third of the projects and tasks they had taken on, boosting the bottom line five to ten points. That approach became so reliable in growing Dolan Media into a $300 million company that the team started doing it within their own operations every few years in what Dolan describes as a rigorous, evidence-based review.

He sums up: "Over time, it's human nature to try new things, to fiddle and experiment. You need to clean house once in a while."

GETTING HOOKED ON PROBLEM SOLVING

Many Fixers grew up or spent their early career in a corporate setting where there was no shortage of needs within projects or divisions. At some point an opportunity was presented to tackle a problem. While serving as President of PepsiCo, Mike Lorelli remembers being sent in to fix another division, Pizza Hut.

The Chairman and CEO of PepsiCo called him and said, "Mike, we know three things about you. You don't know anything about international. You don't know anything about the quick service restaurant industry. But you do have a hell of a reputation for figuring out how to grow stuff, and Pizza Hut's international division is a mess."

Pizza Hut was stuck in neutral, going nowhere. Lorelli was told to "get his butt on a plane and come back with a report thirty days later" on what he found and what he was going to do about it. Inside of twenty-four months, he took Pizza Hut from sixty-eight to ninety-two countries, passing McDonald's in country count and massively boosting cash flow.

Every Fixer has a backstory.

- For John Short, it was launching his career at Citibank where he parachuted in to solve the audit team's challenges when they discovered shady client behavior in Venezuela and then in Hong Kong.

- For Peter Murphy it started in the US Navy, where he saw that flying an ultrasophisticated, complex jet aircraft came with a series of problems to fix.

- For Michelle Barnes it was taking on leadership of Outward Bound, an organization with a wonderful mission that had less-than-wonderful business operations.
- For Mike Bartikoski it was the opportunity at Hershey to restructure offshore operations and restore profitability in Mexico and Brazil.

Fixers figure out they have a knack for solving tough problems ranging from financial distress, to market failure, to bad actors tainting the team. The common denominator is always that the situation is a hot mess, perhaps intractable, and no one else knows how to solve it easily. The challenge proves to be energizing for the rookie Fixer.

The people challenge, the financial intensity, and the negotiations with management or owners, shareholders, lenders, stakeholders—the sheer chaos and messiness of the situation becomes glorious, especially in the rearview mirror, after they've achieved the breakthrough outcome and saved the day.

A HIGH BAR TO ENGAGE

Fixers hold no monopoly—all FABS leaders are problem solvers—it's just that Fixers are drawn primarily to what's already broken, intractably, and there has to be a high bar for them to want to engage. Mike Zawalski, looking at his experiences from Quaker Oats, Ryder, and Coleman, puts it this way: "There's either very acute or significant strategic issues, cultural issues, leadership issues, or operational issues."

Hostess, the 100-year-old bakery behind brands like Ho Hos and Twinkies found itself in need of multiple Fixers when plans and execution continually failed. The company had fallen behind the times, consistently losing money and going into bankruptcy, twice. Everything was broken, except for the fact that millions of people still enjoyed the sugary, indestructible cakes (they'll find intact Twinkies in landfills in the year 2300, no doubt).

Along came Dean Metropoulis. He had spent thirty-five years saving food companies and revitalizing brands including Bumble Bee Tuna, Pabst Blue Ribbon, PAM cooking spray, and Chef Boyardee. Metropoulis led a massive turnaround of Hostess, modernizing factories and centralizing warehouse operations. It now takes just 500 employees in a shiny new plant to crank out one million Twinkies a day, along with three other plants that produce what took fourteen plants and 9,000 workers before.

Like a sprinter getting ready to go for gold, for Fixers the image of the finish line is set from the start. "The desire to fix is very measurable," says Peter Murphy, with over a dozen saves under his belt. "You can understand where you are right now and where you want to go, and you can measure yourself as you move in that direction. It's something that tends to give you—if not instant gratification—as much near-term satisfaction as if you were trying to just move a very successful company forward."

COMPLACENCY IS THE ENEMY

Creating measurable goals and continuing to push the limits is a big driver. "Complacency is the enemy, and it can show up in the form of early success," says COO Mike Bartikoski. "In turning around operations, is an 11 percent improvement enough? Is 35 percent possible? You want to celebrate the wins, and yet still preserve momentum, and ask for more."

How do you keep that momentum going? Fixers don't look back. Perhaps because of the name, we might think the Fixer's goal is to return an organization to some heavenly former state where nothing went wrong, and everyone was happy. In a general sense the Fixer does return the organization to financial health and better morale. Most experts, however, would say there is no "there" to go back to.

"I'm not going to return them to the old former state. Never back to where they were because that's a bad target," says David Johnson. "My biggest enemy is the tendency to look backward. There is so much focus on what was lost, who was fired, and what the company was ten years ago that an inordinate amount of time and energy gets wasted. Usually, though, we can never get back there. We can go here, though, and in many ways here is better and even if it's not better, here is the best we can do."

Of all leadership styles, the Fixer shows the most prominent and visible arc from start to finish, from disaster to success. Almost every Fixer we've ever interviewed described their transcendent moment in the same way, each pointing to the moment when the tides shifted in a positive direction.

THE FIXER FEELS THE TIPPING POINT

Michelle Barnes describes it this way: "I love the day I can feel a tipping point when it moves from me being the evangelist, pushing things, to all of a sudden a couple of employees are on the team and being proactive, bringing their own ideas and changing how they run their department or project. I can always feel it, this tipping point where the momentum goes from you pushing really hard, with everything driven by you and your passion, to instantly leading and helping."

John Short says that, on arrival, a Fixer often has to make bold moves, from shutting down businesses or divisions, to firing people, cutting budgets, and eliminating products. The question then becomes, "How do you keep the management team's focus on the task, and on cooperating and supporting one another to make the business go forward?" He explains that it doesn't happen until people feel like they are at bottom, when they can see this is the go-forward team, and that they are going to make it, together—or not.

"When I see the light bulb come on in their eyes—in the brains of the go-forward management team—that's a great day," Short says.

Michelle Barnes focuses on setting up the organization to continue to build on that initial success, which could include mentoring and eventually passing the baton to another leader to continue to produce longer term results. "Sometimes I will make someone else the Fixer on the team and I'll become the support team. Then they'll keep carrying it on long after I've moved on," she says.

Eric Kish relishes when people start to take steps aligned with his concepts without asking him. "When a new process starts to become a habit in the company, that's the measure of winning for me because my main focus is in changing behaviors. These behaviors have to become habit so people don't even think about them when they make them happen."

To David Johnson it is all about achieving escape velocity. "The plan has worked. You're not done yet, but you can see that your thesis has largely been proven out. The performance is there, and you have enough momentum to carry you forward," he says. Pick your analogy: the team was down 55 to 0, or the patient was on his deathbed, but when that moment of escape velocity is achieved, Johnson says it's a wonderful feeling.

When the fix is complete, it can be a bittersweet moment. There is great satisfaction in a job well done, but the victory can be mixed with a sense of sadness, because now it's time to move on. The intensity of working around the clock with a dedicated team comes to an end.

"My worst day is the day I leave," Johnson says. "You build relationships, you have seen a company through its darkest hour. You have promoted a few people and put them on a new career trajectory, and then one day it's over and you're not the center of the world and the phone doesn't ring fifty times and you don't have fifteen things to do. The adrenaline stops all at once. You're on a constant feed and then it's done. You're happy, but it is crushing."

And so it's time for the next fix, the next adrenaline rush. Perhaps like Johnson, the veteran Fixer will take time off for a system reset and reboot, so that they can jump into the next crisis fresh, clear, and eager for the new.

The Fixer Leader		
• Linear	• Adrenaline Junkie	• Observant
• Nimble	• Open Minded	• Intense
• Expeditious	• Impatient	• Straight Shooter
• Laser Focused	• Practical	• Heroic

In the Trenches with Fixers

*"If I put a Fixer into one of my companies
and it's not broken, he'll break it.
Just so he can fix it."*
—JIM DOLAN, Dolan Ventures

Fixers run into burning buildings. How do they do that time after time, seemingly emerging unscathed while consistently delivering winning saves for companies, teams, and investors?

This section called In the Trenches is a deeper dive into Fixers' winning habits. What they do from the get-go, how they create ongoing improvement, and when and how they will exit once the crisis is past. Finally, our take on these special ops leaders can't overlook what happens when the wrong leader shows up, the Fixer driven to excess.

SETTING THE TONE ON DAY ONE

Day one for any Fixer stepping into an organization, division, or project is critical in setting the tone for the work ahead. CEO Mike Lorelli sees many organizations facing crisis falling down not just in big ways like revenues and profits, but also in consistent operational excellence. On his first day kicking off a turnaround of a manufacturing plant, Lorelli got up way before the crack of dawn and drove through three states to be the first person at the plant—a move that caught everyone by surprise, but mattered a lot to him as CEO.

"Boy, does that send an electrifying signal through the company and that travels through the hallways pretty quickly," he says adding that it was crystal clear to the team that the CEO is the first guy in the building, and it's important to him to walk the plant floor, say hello to everybody, make sure the machines are starting up and everything is running smoothly, and be there to talk through any issues as they come up. Sure enough, a lot of other people started showing up early and Lorelli notes that even small moves like that led to long-term productivity gains.

John Short says his first move is to "talk less, listen more, learn, ask a lot of questions, and understand the industry." It can be easy for a successful leader to charge in as if they know everything and are going to solve all your problems—something Short refers to as "savior syndrome," but it's critical to keep an open mind.

Being respectful of the history of the organization is key. "Turnaround situations are emotionally painful for people," says David Johnson who knows that stress levels can often be off the charts, so he makes a point to be generous with his time. "I always like to go to stakeholders by expressing my sympathy for the situation they're in and giving them some time to vent before we move on to how we're going to fix it. They need that."

Part turnaround expert, part therapist, part detective, the Fixer meets and ideally bonds with team members throughout the organization to uncover the full realm of challenges. Ultimately, the intelligence from management to the shop floor to the administrative team can be gold mines of information and insight, adding up to a collective genius playbook for saving and reviving the organization. This investigative work also reveals deeper issues, whether it's a breakdown in supply chain and distribution channels, team turnover, or financial mismanagement.

In his practice of walking the shop floor to ask people what they see and what their main areas of concern are, Dick Lindenmuth immediately worked quickly to build trust among the team. "Staff might say if we had better lighting on the production line, quality control would go up," he says. "For a hundred bucks you put in a couple of lamps and quickly demonstrate that you listen to people and take action. At the same time the lighting's better and the environment and quality control probably went up." He says it's these small, positive actions that add up while setting the stage for future bigger and more meaningful change.

When Lindenmuth stepped into a family-owned manufacturing company in California, equipment was so broken that the plant was shut down, operations and accounting were a mess, and the owners were facing millions of dollars in losses. He quickly found that people issues were a major component.

"The former managers only went onto the shop floor to fire somebody," he says. One day walking down the production line, he came across a grandmother—a Hindu woman who didn't speak English. "I had been to the Golden Temple in Punjab, India, so I just put my hands together in a prayer symbol of respect and nodded," he remembers. Through a translator he called her grandmother and thanked her for what she was doing. She broke down in tears, saying that she had been there for fourteen years, and no one had ever communicated with her.

THE GO-FORWARD TEAM

Once the assessment is complete, there comes a point when it's time to start laying out the road map for taking the business forward. That means not just settling on strategy and tactics, but also a go-forward team, which can be a rocky road for the Fixer.

In the early stages of stepping into a troubled business, downsizing or restructuring loom over the proceedings. It's not a comfortable feeling for workers, and the divide within an organization can quickly become evident.

"Everybody's looking over their shoulder, thinking, I'm either going to leave and find a job on my own because I can or I'm going to try to figure out how to undermine and kill the other guys so that I survive the grim reaper," Short describes. You'd think you jumped into an episode of *Survivor*, where it's everyone for themselves, but uncertainty is inextricably weaved into the early part of saving any organization.

The Fixer must figure out how to bring the team together, and Short makes a point to be direct every step of the way, telling people to "think big, work small, be frank, fight hard for your position, but when a decision is made, we all get into the same canoe and paddle in the same direction."

Despite best efforts, even the best leaders and motivators find that not everyone wants to come along for the ride. "These are high-pressure situations where people are asked to do more in a shorter period of time than they probably have ever done in their careers," Short says. After getting through the tough part of repositioning, restructuring, and identifying who he wants on the team, he says his worst day is when somebody comes in and gives notice. It can feel like a punch to the gut, even for veteran leaders, as they work to bring about some form of stability. It's never a given that all the key players will stay on board.

Fixers often walk into a situation where they are met with a wall of stubbornness and resistance from those who see the leader as a temporary fixture—someone to be tolerated and simply outlasted. In serving as Chief Operating Officer, when Mike Bartikoski implements a new system in a manufacturing plant, he says, "I've actually heard supervisors say to operators when they thought I was out of earshot, 'Yeah, do it that way while they're here. When they go away, you can go back to doing it the way we've always done.'"

This led Bartikoski to something he calls his Rule of 13. "Unless you repeat a direction at least thirteen times, people aren't going to really buy into it," he says, noting that in running operations around the world, he appreciates the value of repeat communication regardless of culture, location, or rank.

Ironically, he has found the value of repetition is often lost the higher up you go. "When you're dealing with folks on the front line and you have a different crew day in and day out, repeating direction is pretty clear," he says. "Once you become a director, vice president, or CEO, the thought that you only have to say it once for people to buy in becomes ever more tempting. But you need to repeat and be consistent about those things that are important, particularly those things that embody change."

One of the main things that John Short communicates over and over is to work small, meaning that every member of the leadership team needs to be intimately involved in the day-to-day execution by leading in the trenches—not by "managing." No ivory towers allowed.

Encouraging entrenched management to get out of their corner offices and embed themselves with employees and customers can open up new opportunities to restore ongoing improvement. Dick Lindenmuth gave an example of a manufacturing plant where he happened to see a worker demonstrating a safer way to complete a process. He jumped into his car, bought a $50 Walmart gift card, came back and took a picture with the person, thanking them for a job well done. "The individual appreciated it, and the tone completely changed to it being a fun place to work, or at least a good place to work," he says.

A LITTLE LESS CHAOS, PLEASE

Like any other profession, Fixers come in flavors from inspiring to so-so, where the outcome is mediocre at best. Worse is the so-called Fixer who can't get past the slash-and-burn page in the playbook. Under the guise of saving the organization, wholesale slaughter could be taking place within the employee ranks. We need to look at someone like Al Dunlap to get at the kind of evil excesses that are possible when a Fixer runs amok.

When the Sunbeam board of directors called Dunlap to take over the failing manufacturer of kitchen blenders and appliances in the mid-1990s, Wall Street took notice and shares jumped up. Known for his ability to rejigger organizations, usually by way of massive layoffs and factory closures, Dunlap had earned the nickname "Chainsaw Al."

At Scott Paper he paid off the company's $2.5 billion in debt, in part by firing 11,200 people, fully one-third of the workforce. While some praised him for being able to boost shareholder value, others questioned if it was a hoax—a form of financial engineering that, while maximizing short-term gains, was at the expense of the long-term health of the company.

Despite the doubters, Dunlap was brought in to save the day. He showed no mercy, axing half of Sunbeam's 12,000 employees. Shareholders loved it, until the SEC got wind of fraud, at which point it all came crashing down. The SEC filed a complaint against the company, saying that "at least $62 million of Sunbeam's reported $189 million in income for the year did not comply" with accounting rules. Reports circulated that a financial analyst confronted Dunlap at an investor meeting, prompting Dunlap to grab the analyst, place a hand over his mouth, and say, "You son of a bitch. If you want to come after me, I'll come after you twice as hard."

From *People* magazine's description of him as "The Terminator" to *Time's* "World's Worst Bosses" to *Fast Company's* list of potential CEO psychopaths, Dunlap was finally called out. He settled with the SEC, paying a $500,000 fine while being permanently banned as an officer or director at any publicly traded company. Sunbeam restated its financials and entered Chapter 11 bankruptcy protection in 2001.

Even among Fixers acting with integrity, there can be the temptation to go too far. "Once the problem is fixed, the tiger team becomes dangerous because they almost attack each other," says Dick Lindenmuth, veteran of twenty-three company saves.

CEO Michelle Barnes acknowledges there is a point when she needs to step away. "I'm all in," but adds, "if I was at a company for more than a year, I think people would ask, 'When is Michelle going on vacation?' We need a little downtime to process. I don't think the intensity of a lot of Fixers is healthy long term. It's just too much, too fast."

In reviving flailing manufacturing companies, David Sheehan realizes that he's essentially working himself out of the job by improving processes and decision-making, while instilling lean principles among the leadership team and workers. He recognizes that some Fixers get caught in a bizarre type of tug-of-war.

"On one hand you could say a turnaround person like me is an adrenaline junkie always wanting a new project or an important, urgent crisis. The messier the better," he says.

The flip side of the coin is that while Sheehan likes a mess, he also hates chaos and wants to turn chaos into a fully functioning organization. Once order has been restored, there is this pull to start again, so he says "the worst thing is if you have a person who likes chaos and serves to keep it going."

THE WHITE KNIGHT

The urgency and intensity Fixers bring is exactly what is needed while the clock is ticking, deadlines are looming, and an organization needs to be brought back to health pronto. Baked into that, however, is a knowing, an intuition of when it's time to move on. Beyond executing on a plan with a thoroughness that stands a good chance of ensuring the organization's viability, the Fixer typically puts in place or reinforces a capable management team that can continue to drive forward within new controls and better structure.

Understanding that once the fix is complete, she will move to her next challenge, Michelle Barnes says it's important that people don't see her as the white knight. "It has to feel like it's owned by the team," she says adding that her job is to credit the people on the team, build them up, and empower them to feel like they turned things around.

Creating consistency within the organization and cohesion among the team is essential for future progress. In a *Wall Street Journal* article by Sam Walker, author of *The Captain Class: A New Theory of Leadership,* Walker describes US Naval commanders relying on a concept of "battle rhythm" where they "determine the tempo of briefings, drills, and even sleep routines," ultimately working to help the crew prevail in crisis. He points to Alan Mulally's technique at Ford during a massive downturn, which was publicly described as working to eliminate distractions and internal feuding.

"Mulally instituted regular Thursday meetings in which phones, mean jokes, opinions, side conversations and turf battles were banned, and bathroom breaks were discouraged," Walker explains. "To improve decision-making, he prodded executives to bring along more data and be more forthcoming with bad news." The end result? Ford's value increased by more than $45 billion from his arrival in 2006 to exit in 2014.

The Fixer must also foster an environment where good decision-making practices are sustained. Peter Murphy imposes a rule on all of his managers that no important decisions can be made on a Friday afternoon. This might seem like a crazy concept when we live in a 24/7 culture, but Murphy gave reasons why the Friday afternoon habit still works. "On Monday you know that on Tuesday you can keep talking, reacting, pivoting, for one. And on Friday, everyone on the team is thinking about their weekend, the family, the soccer game you have to get your kid to," he says, noting that even within tech cultures where people routinely work weekends, big decision-making is reserved for weekdays.

Ultimately, the team is encouraged to share ideas and take action on them. At the beginning of an assignment, Michelle Barnes gives the team hope and confidence, showing them that she is in charge and that the ship can be turned. But once momentum and buy-in is achieved, she moves into more of a coach role so that when she leaves, she's in the rearview mirror and the team can embrace their own competence and capabilities, confident in the future ahead.

The need for expert Fixers is unquenchable, as we inevitably move in cycles from smooth sailing to crisis. Whether it's financial problems, a sudden market shift, revenue going down, or a loss of momentum, business as usual won't work, and it's talented Fixers that are the foundation from which seemingly impossible-to-solve disaster can instead lead to sustained periods of newfound wealth. Choose your poison. Recession. Corruption. Malfeasance or fraud. When the right Fixer shows up and works their magic, it's a relief and you can bask in the newfound feeling of prosperity and forward movement.

You Know You Are a Fixer If . . .

✓ You are drawn to helping troubled, dysfunctional, and even toxic organizations or situations.

✓ You see what's broken, and you know how to turn it around.

✓ You can't help yourself: Chaos must turn to order.

✓ Velocity is your middle name.

✓ You drive for measurable improvement.

✓ You explore triggers that will have the best ROI.

✓ You implement controls.

✓ You make decisions quickly.

✓ Your mindset is financial and analytical.

✓ You are candid and direct.

✓ You have a knack for helping people see why change must happen and the important role they play.

✓ You might be questioned as being the enemy, but could leave as the hero.

✓ Your superpower is calm in the face of chaos.

✓ You are energized by intensity and urgency.

✓ You look for your next challenge once a situation is back to health.

2.
THE ARTIST

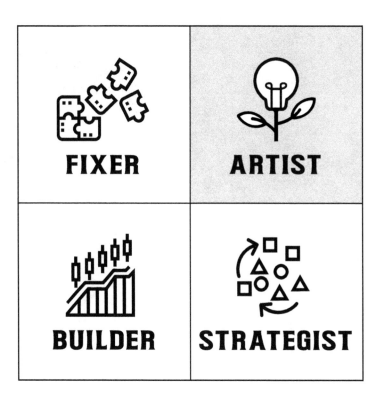

FIXER

ARTIST

BUILDER

STRATEGIST

An Artist Story: Composing a Masterpiece

It was 2004 and John Wu, a thirty-two-year-old indie singer-songwriter, had big ambitions. He had a new idea for an album that he had never seen done before, and as an independent artist with no label backing him, he was convinced it would be a game changer for his career.

He hired a big-time producer and a studio engineer, shoveling out $1,000 a day to make his dream come true. There was just one little problem: with no concept of budgeting or how to track expenses, when he looked at his bank account one day, he did a double take at his remaining cash: $144. He was broke.

Wu did not have a traditional music background. He had studied engineering at the University of Illinois where he got the chance to work at the National Center for Supercomputing Applications with the team that launched the first web browser, which would eventually become Netscape. He had a love for creating and building things. As a kid, his mom would find him tearing apart alarm clocks or other electronics to see how they worked.

When Wu started playing music at the age of five, he discovered his path to freedom. Freedom of time. Freedom to express himself as an artist. Taking the route of a singer-songwriter felt like it brought the right elements together, so he was content making $30,000 a year on his own, which was more than enough to support his bachelor life in Champaign, Illinois.

It wasn't all smooth sailing though and the moment his bank account plummeted to zero turned his life upside down. A new-found motivation emerged. "It's like the doctor saying you have high cholesterol. You aren't motivated until you hit bottom," Wu explains. What seemed like his worst moment led to a crash course in business and changed the trajectory of his life. He read hundreds of books on making and managing money. *The Millionaire Next Door*, *Rich Dad's CASHFLOW Quadrant*, and *The 4-Hour Workweek* opened up a new world for him as a recurring theme emerged: passive income.

Assets that produce income was a new concept for Wu, but he did know about royalties from the music business. He thought back to when he opened for a major label artist where the lead singer would fly coach, and the drummer first class. He found it strange that the lead singer—the famous one with a big fan following—was the one flying coach. It turned out, however, that the drummer was the guy who wrote the songs. While the lead singer only got paid for the gigs he performed, the drummer went to the bank every time the song was in a movie or on the radio. He got paid while he slept.

The big question Wu kept coming back to was how he could maintain an income stream without having to work constantly. How to enjoy his freedom and lifestyle while staying true to his art. He was already getting a little jaded with how business operated for musicians. Every decision in the studio revolved around how to make more money. He remembers shortening intros because the producers told him that most pop songs would have already hit the vocals at that point.

He couldn't help but think of how, against all odds, "Bohemian Rhapsody," a six-minute song (virtually a lifetime in the music business) or twenty-minute-plus songs by Pink Floyd won the hearts of fans by focusing on the authenticity of the music. It seemed to him that real success came by directly reaching audiences or solving a problem, where money was merely a by-product.

A CHANCE MEETING WITH CD BABY

One of the most influential people in Wu's life was Derek Sivers, founder of CD Baby, a famous online seller of independent music. In 2003 Wu attended a music conference in Nashville where Sivers was a featured speaker. Listening to Sivers on stage, Wu would later realize that Sivers's story and the ideas he shared would serve as a tipping point for Wu's ultimate success in business.

Like Wu, Derek Sivers was a musician and started CD Baby as a website to sell his own music. A multimillion-dollar company grew up much by accident as more and more friends asked Sivers to sell their music on his site. He was the first person to introduce Wu to the idea that programming is much like song writing, but it's focused more on the technical creation versus writing a hit song.

While traveling and performing in shows around the country, John Wu had drawn on his engineering and programming background to create a website designed for him and his musician friends. The site used algorithms to calculate the cost of gas to drive to a venue and the fastest way to get there, factoring in the time difference if you were booking a gig in another state. Wu did not design the site with a commercial end in mind, but rather to solve a problem he often felt as a roaming entertainer. And then the market weighed in.

More and more people discovered his site called Travelmath. He got emails from people asking why they couldn't directly book a flight or a hotel after mapping out their optimal route. Wu couldn't understand why anyone would want that. The airlines and hotels would happily take their calls, and he was perfectly fine with the functionality the site provided.

The suggestions kept coming and he started wondering maybe this was kind of like playing a live performance. When a musician is on stage, the audience guides you. Good artists will even change their set or flow of music on the fly to cater to the mood of the audience. That was the moment when Wu got the idea to expand into more of a travel site than something just for musicians.

Travelmath had turned into a business, and before too long it was grossing millions of dollars in ad revenue. We think of John Wu, an Artist leader, as an example of the power that comes from those who lead first and foremost through innovation and creative expression.

This club is not limited to the mega famous like Elon Musk or Thomas Edison. John Wu is not known to the general public, but his unique form of leadership allows him to bring about an artistry that disrupts industries and conventional ways of thinking. He sees through clutter to identify new ideas and opportunities. Artist leaders are not just technologists. Artistry and innovation are core to brilliant marketing, financial engineering, social media, governance, scientific advance, philanthropy, and every other human endeavor.

For Wu it was audience feedback at Travelmath that started him on his road to reinvention. As a musician, he learned that he liked songwriting a lot more than live performance. In business, he was sure he was not going to be a showy CEO up on stage in front of thousands of people.

Just as with songwriting, he loved designing and coming up with ideas for making software work better. He knew he wanted a business that would be as close to self-sustaining as possible. A business built around systems, automation, and search engine optimization that would give him *freedom*—a key word for John and all other Artist leaders—to continue to create and scale without having to be on the phone with vendors or customers every day.

With these core principles in mind, Travelmath exploded into a destination site used by millions of travelers and the biggest airlines to assist their customers with travel plans. Wu had what he describes as thousands of discussions with himself—days and nights, pacing back and forth in his living room—while making sure to document every idea that popped into his head on how to tweak the website or grow the company.

"I'll have hundreds of ideas and I'll just be thinking that every single one of those will be great because I'm an optimist by nature," Wu says. "But when I go back, I'll see okay, nine out of ten times the ideas will not do much. But roughly one out of ten, I'll hit a home run."

Wu and his team don't have time to pursue every idea, so he goes for the easiest ideas with the biggest potential return. Early on, everyone in the industry said page speed was not a factor in how a web page would rank in an online search. But Wu had a gut feeling that maybe it could be, so he decided to try to boost the speed anyway. Within twenty-four hours, traffic and revenue had doubled. He says the feeling he got when he saw the results was the exact same as writing a really great song.

PLAYING POKER, JUST A LITTLE
TOO AGGRESSIVELY

Wu's reputation was growing in software circles as an innovative designer and website builder. At one point he was walking the long aisles of the annual travel industry conference and his phone dinged with a text from a friend inviting him to the penthouse suite of the hotel for a poker game.

"I loved poker, so I immediately said yes and walked into a room with some of the biggest travel industry CEOs," Wu recalls. "I bought in, and played aggressively, taking out the host within the first couple hands. What I quickly realized was that no one actually knew how to play poker. They weren't there to beat each other, but to just network and talk business."

His friends still joke about his faux pas, but, at the time, Wu couldn't believe that as salespeople were walking the conference floor, these CEOs—merciless competitors in the marketplace—were sitting around talking and having fun. It was a lesson for Wu on collaboration, and, ultimately, it was that poker game that led to his next business venture.

Trippy, a site designed to answer and collect travel questions from around the globe, had been founded by one of his fellow poker players who already had successfully built and sold a company to Tripadvisor. When a deal to sell the company fell through, the founder approached Wu to see if he wanted to take over the website.

Acquiring Trippy made sense to him. It presented him with a challenge to develop a new and different approach to revamp the site, rejigger the team, and scale in a way that had not been done before. Assessing the business through that lens, Wu purchased the assets, and today Wu's businesses collectively reach over 100 million people

with a team of a dozen designers, programmers, search engine opti-
mizers, and travel writers.

"In the same way that a traditional company might have millions
of customers, I may have millions of people using a tool that I've created," he says.

John Wu is relentless in thinking about what will allow him to
maintain a lean organization while creating more artificial intelligence (AI) applications in order to serve millions and millions more
people. He explains the need to create systems in the same way
McDonald's has systems for creating products or managing quality
control.

Traditionally companies would train employees to do a certain
task. For Wu, if he could train someone to do a task over and over
again, his mindset is to program a system to do the same thing
instead. Software has given developers an ability to leverage AI and
machine learning to make this possible. Wu still very much needs
team members, but his leadership style has prompted the creation of
a much more democratic organization at Trippy and Travelmath. He
describes his team as being made up of specialized talent that is self-
starting, self-motivated, and able to organize themselves and develop
their own education as needs arise.

"If you're that kind of person that has built your own expertise
around an area that you particularly enjoy and are good at, then that
skill becomes very valuable to me," Wu says. "Now I can benefit from
someone who's invested a lot of their own time becoming really good
at something. I just have to have enough knowledge around each area
of expertise to know that they're good at it. It's hard to become that
really top expert that's put in thousands of hours."

Building the system behind Trippy is fun for Wu. "It doesn't feel
like work. People understood it when I was playing guitar. They were

like, 'Oh yeah, you're playing,' when I was also working on an album and making money. Now, when I say I'm playing with Trippy, most people respond, 'That doesn't sound like fun to be sitting in front of the computer.' But to me it's the same process."

He points to the holy grail or what he calls "the inspiration kick." It's what happens when people talk about an idea coming to them in the shower or flowing out of their subconscious. As a musician, John could spend day after day sitting, working on monotonous tasks like scales and techniques to produce a hit song, when in reality he says, "The best songs are the ones that literally just flow through you from the universe. They come out in an hour."

It's seeing the fruits of those acts of creativity that energizes him. While he was marching around Walt Disney World with his kids, he pulled up his phone to check on his website stats and had his third highest revenue day ever. He was gone for a week and the systems were working.

Another trip did not go so smoothly. Sipping a pina colada at a friend's wedding in Hawaii turned into being glued to his computer when he discovered that his systems had blown up. Wu was the one who had to fix it.

"A couple people can build a billion-dollar company," Wu says. "Instagram is a good example. As a small team, if something went wrong because they were growing so quickly, one of the guys would pull out a laptop and fix it even at dinner. But that's because he would be fixing a system or improving a system, not trying to answer emails from 10,000 people."

NONCONFORMISTS, STEP RIGHT UP

Wu says the core of being an Artist leader is nonconformist. Many of his friends thought it was weird that he was working on business when he liked to sleep in, but he knew he was driven to generate passive income. He discovered his strength is more about identifying a technical element that has big returns. It's not rocket science or never-been-done-before stuff, he says, but rather just using data in a useful way.

"I was never the best guitar player," Wu says. "I was proficient. And I am for sure not the top programmer. There are a million better people out there. I've worked with the rock star developers that know all the latest JavaScript, CSS, and really complicated server stuff, but the audience doesn't care how beautiful your code looks if it doesn't solve a problem for them."

In ten years where will John Wu be? "Right here," he says. "I'm a creator. I'm a composer. If I continue to get better and better at that, I can actually create a truly global and amazing AI for travel that can really answer all your trip planning questions and help plan your trip."

That won't stop his parents from worrying, of course. Ever since his bank account hit rock bottom as a young musician, Wu says they still come up with ridiculous scenarios where history could repeat itself. His response is indicative of a true Artist: "I could lose everything and walk out the door with just a shirt on my back, and I could build it all back again. It's not what I have and it's not the technology or the people; it's the songwriting. It's the composing."

The Artist Leadership Mode

Creation is mantra for the Artist.

We all have a creative spark, but what sets the Artist leader apart is that it's *the* vital necessity, which can crowd out all other ambitions, considerations, reason, success, or sanity. Mozart admitted he wrote music "the way cows pissed." It just happened. It was unstoppable. It was the motivating force driving his existence.

The Artist leader looks at the world as their canvas. Company, project, application, product, service, financial model, brand positioning, operational strategy, campaign, tag line, algorithm, network, community, political movement, nation state—you name it, the Artist seeks to have their creative stamp on it. It is canvas to paint. Clay to sculpt. Even if the canvas has already been sketched, the Artist will re-envision, re-create, reconfigure, copy, steal, or add fresh perspective. Theirs is the vision that shines brightest.

Jeff Leitner has spent his career solving complex problems and bringing social innovation to organizations ranging from the US Department of State to NASA, Panera, Starbucks, and the Dalai Lama Center for Peace and Education. He sees the Artist leader as more empirical, meaning they learn from creating and watching how something behaves, as opposed to being analytical, working on homework problems, and projecting whether or not it will work.

"There are people who work in the lab and there are empiricists like me who just build stuff, put it out there and see how it interacts with the real world," Leitner says. "That's how innovation works, right? When the world tells everyone that they should learn to prototype, Artists say sure, call it what you want. I've got stuff to construct."

There is an insatiable urge to create. Psychologist Tim Tate, who counsels some of the best mountain climbers in the world, which is its own form of creative expression, has been reported saying, "They can't help but do what they do." That's the mark of the Artist—at risk of life itself, they will persevere to follow a calling, to get to the outer edge of the thing.

What each Artist chooses to create—that canvas varies widely. "My art results in new and innovative technology products," says Dean Samuels, who has been an interim Chief Information Officer for many firms. "It is original even if there was something on the canvas before."

While Samuels still dedicates some time to optimizing servers, architecting for the cloud, reducing IT costs, or attracting talented staff, he views those duties as mostly operational. What gets him excited is reimagining technology to grow business through innovation. The best IT is no longer just an equalizer. It's a strategic enabler. It's about leveraging technology in creative ways to dominate with an unfair advantage. Walmart did it in retail, and every industry is blending IT and business to bring about disruption and new ways of thinking. Samuels is constantly on the lookout for emerging trends and areas of opportunity.

For Chief Marketing Officer Joshua Katz, the canvas is all about building a brand and creating a marketing strategy. Katz says that means ignoring all of the noise and asking what's the one thing that's going to make the end user stand up and pay attention? What is the value proposition that you have that no one else has? What is the way to communicate that value that's going to resonate?

Katz, who has been called on to build brands from TiVo, to Cartoon Network, VH1, and the ABC Family channel (now called Freeform), has seen many brands go out of their way to explain themselves and say how great they are, but forget that the end user is the one that they should be talking to.

Innovation in consumer product design and performance is the driver for Sir James Dyson. Frustrated with the constant clogs and dust that came from using the popular Hoover vacuum, he spent fifteen years iterating through 5,000 prototypes to invent a bagless cleaner powered by cyclone technology. Dyson employs 12,000 people and is consistently re-envisioning how products from vacuum cleaners to air purifiers to hair dryers could function better.

"I don't really look at markets at all. Otherwise, I would have never gone into hand drying," said Dyson in a podcast interview with LinkedIn cofounder Reid Hoffman. "When we have technology we feel could do something interesting, we go into that field. It's entirely technology- and product-led. It's not led by market size. Hand dryers are not a sexy business, but we had the technology which did it better."

FOR RENEGADES, NOT BUSINESS AS USUAL

The Artist is a leader, or more likely the anti-leader. They can lead the troops so long as everyone understands they'll lead by being the renegade, the perpetual outsider. They are out on the edge, curious, and pushing against norms and business as usual. The Artist seeks change, not for change's sake but because they see something better. And that's where the difficulty begins, because most people resist change, even at the cost of their lives. Research on heart bypass patients shows that 90 percent will not change their lifestyle even when told they'll die if they don't.

Some Artist leaders have the ability to work for "the man"—IBM, GM, Siemens, Oracle, city hall, the federal government, or any other bureaucracy. But it might just kill them, unless the organization is open to innovation. The Artist has to be able to leave their stamp.

Large organizations that truly nurture the Artist leader within are rare, but they can dramatically outperform their stodgy peers. PWC's annual Global Innovation 1000 study ranks the top thousand public companies based on research and development spend. The findings? Standout innovation is not a function of who can throw the most cash at R&D. Since the first study in 2006, no relationship has ever been found between innovation spending and financial performance.

PWC reports, "What matters instead is the particular combination of talent, knowledge, team structures, tools, and processes—the capabilities—that successful companies put together to enable their innovation efforts, and thus create products and services they can successfully take to market."

While the thousand companies collectively spent $782 billion on R&D in 2018, just eighty-eight were deemed to be high-leverage innovators, meaning that despite having less outlay on R&D as a percentage of sales, these organizations still managed to outperform their peers on key measures of financial success. The best performers include Artist leaders nurtured within a culture that aligns innovation with overall business strategy.

INDEPENDENCE FROM WITHIN, OR WITHOUT

Without an outlet or maybe even a side hustle for the Artist leader to express themselves, they could spontaneously combust from thwarted creative ambition or ability to execute on their big ideas. The alternative for the Artist leader is to do their own thing.

"People have asked me many times to involve myself with public companies, public boards, and so on, and my answer to them is at my age if I wanted to be that regulated, I'd simply take Metamucil," says Bernie Rudnick, who has helped found dozens of medical device and healthcare companies, producing value in the hundreds of millions of dollars.

For many Artist leaders, creating something that they can do on their own terms that fits with their outlook on the world—what they stand for at their core—is a powerful driver. Chris McAllister spent fifteen years in retail management. But there came a day when he couldn't get out of his head his fond memories from his college years, working for a mom-and-pop art supplies store that quickly grew from eight to fifty stores. That struck him as incredibly energizing.

McAllister decided to give it a go and set out to tackle the real estate world, getting licensed and buying three RE/MAX franchises between 2003 and 2005. By 2008 all hell broke loose in the real estate market, and with revenues vanishing, his company filed for bankruptcy.

McAllister was back at square one but took the opportunity to think about how he could create something that could grow and be sustained over the long term. That was the spark of what became a multistate real estate company that would create a holistic community between renters, buyers, and investors. "What I wanted didn't exist, so I built it myself," he says.

Clothing designer Eileen Fisher recalled the start of her career in a *New York Times* interview: "I was trying to work as a designer and trying to look like a designer. But I was struggling to put myself together. It was just overwhelming. I felt clothes were too complicated, especially women's clothes, always changing. I just needed to look good, and I needed to not think too much about it."

Feeling there was a gap in the marketplace set the foundation for the creation of her now $500 million fashion brand. Fisher's Artist leader imprint on the company is direct when it comes to defining core values: timeless clothing designs, sustainability, and simplicity. She has spent thirty years directing modestly and collaboratively, never needing to be defined as a traditional boss.

"I don't think being a boss is my strength," she says. "I think of myself as leading through the idea, trying to help people understand what I'm trying to do, or what the project is about, and engaging them. I always think about leading through listening."

Fisher's awareness of her strengths was important in how she designed the company, choosing to forgo the CEO title, saying that she is "a little uncomfortable with that title." She used to call herself the Chief Creative Officer since she often leads from the creative sense, but today wears the title Chairwoman of the Board. She insists, however, that title is not how she defines herself, and it's more about what she is creating: "I wanted to create a place where people weren't powering over people. Where people were kind, and people were together, and shared."

The Artist mindset is wired for breakthrough, for the jump, the revolution, the discontinuous leap. Writer, poet, and deep thinker Ursula Le Guin reminds us that "any human power can be resisted and changed by human beings. Resistance and change often begin in art."

During her acceptance speech for her second National Book Award she continued to build on this: "Hard times are coming, when we'll be wanting the voices of writers who can see alternatives to how we live now, can see through our fear-stricken society and its obsessive technologies to other ways of being, and even imagine real grounds for hope. We'll need writers who can remember freedom—poets, visionaries—realists of a larger reality."

REACHING THE BREAKING POINT: TAKING ON GENOCIDE

The year 2006 marked the twelfth anniversary in Rwanda since the genocidal rampage against the Tutsi resulted in one million dead. The ruling Hutu used the army and militia to carry out organized slaughter over a hundred-day period, even encouraging Hutu civilians to attack, rape, maim, and kill their Tutsi neighbors. The carnage ended only because a superior military force led by Paul Kagame was successful in capturing the capital city of Kigali.

The twelfth anniversary also marked the moment when David Ormesher decided he'd finally had enough.

Ormesher's day job was running a digital marketing firm he founded after getting fed up with how a company he worked for treated their employees and made management decisions. At the time, his goal was to create a successful, high-performing, and profitable firm with a culture of meritocracy. Through the years his motive evolved, however, and soon he felt it was the responsibility of a leader to create opportunities for others.

In serving on boards of large nonprofit relief and development agencies that were doing work around the world, Ormesher felt the model wasn't sustainable. They were all funded and implemented from the outside. He had a vision for a different approach. As a leader calling his own shots, he felt he should be working with others who felt similarly empowered to own their destiny.

His thoughts moved to help the war-torn population in Rwanda regain peace and amity, while building new opportunities and a strong economy from the ground up. "If I could find a way to enable my colleagues, my peers, if you will, to grow their businesses to accelerate growth faster, it would have a much more meaningful long-term impact on that country and the lives of citizens," he says.

In 2008 Ormesher took action, traveling repeatedly to Rwanda over the next eighteen months. In the beginning, he wasn't sure what to do and "needed to learn the rhythm and cadence of Kigali," to discover the right model and content for an organization geared toward empowering new companies to launch, and existing businesses to grow and expand. Beyond structure and sequence of a program, Ormesher knew he must have clear expectations and measures of success. He made a promise to himself. For a minimum of ten years he would travel to Rwanda four times each year to coach company owners. That was the beginning of his new organization, Bigger Future.

In 2018 Ormesher met his promise, having made forty trips over ten years, back and forth from the US to Rwanda to coach and train 300 business owners. One of those success stories is Azizi Life, a company that brings together cohorts of women in villages to teach them how to make Rwandan specialty products that are then sold online. In the process of selling physical products, the team recognized an unforeseen opportunity for growth.

The story of these women and the products they were creating by hand was starting to boost local tourism. A completely new experience-based line of business spun out of this insight and gave visitors the opportunity to spend a day or week in the villages working alongside the women, learning about village life and the unique culture of Rwanda. This women-owned and women-managed company now employs hundreds of full-time artisans.

Ormesher's vision, follow-through, and execution was not only a commercial success, but more significantly saved and improved the lives of thousands.

CHALLENGING THE STATUS QUO

There is a status quo that is aggrieving to the Artist's eye.

The instinct of this leader is to challenge and test the limits, then paint a picture—a vision—of what can be, to inspire others to come along with them. The Artist leader has an ability to tap into and mobilize deeper values, motivations, and shared purpose—something that has been the backbone of successful movements throughout history.

"I like being a challenger. I like to try to change the world order, and I find that to be both very motivating for me, and also I think it's very powerful as a story or a tool for motivating teams of people. If we're going to make a difference, we have to inspire others to lead," says Dave Friedman who, like Dave Ormesher, found a calling beyond his nine-to-five work life that caused him to create what hadn't existed before.

When Friedman's autistic son, Matt, turned fourteen, his school began leading transition planning to help determine what a child with autism would do after high school. "The unemployment rate of adults with autism is 80 percent, and of the 20 percent that are working, they're mostly in low skilled jobs stocking shelves or cleaning tables," Friedman says. It was a bitter reality.

"Matt is high functioning," Friedman explains. "He's talented in a lot of ways, but he wasn't going to be successful in college. He doesn't have the executive functioning and social skills to work in that complex environment." Despite college not being in the cards, Dave and his wife noticed a variety of tasks that Matt was good at. There had to be a job out there for him. Years of research followed, trying to find an opening that fit with Matt's skills, but it became more and more apparent that one didn't seem to exist.

Friedman's own leadership style was evolving at the same time. But a common theme persisted: he was drawn to finding ways to disrupt an industry. "I like to lead from this idea of we are here now to drive change. Even if it's hard and processes are messed up, it's because we are trying to create something that doesn't exist," he says.

His earlier career showed both his Artist side, as well as a strong dose of Fixer. He was hired by a hotshot internet consultancy, and when the internet bubble burst, the company became a roller coaster, free-falling from 2,000 people down to thirty-five. From that low point, Friedman worked to regain business, making acquisitions and taking the team back up to 1,500. From that success he decided to jump to an old-line company, Sears, not foreseeing how it would change his and his son Matt's life forever.

As President of Marketing for Sears, Friedman oversaw iconic brands like Craftsman, Kenmore, and DieHard. At the time, Sears produced ninety million circulars (freestanding advertising inserts) a week. Staff members spent their days laying out descriptions and graphics for the ads, proofing and cutting images, and checking pricing week in and week out. Friedman thought to himself, Matt could do this.

Once the idea was planted, he started seeing opportunity all over the place. "I remembered back to when I was at Razorfish where we had a huge group of people setting up ad campaigns and doing basic reporting and optimization. You hired people, telling them you're coming to work in an ad agency, when in reality they were really going to enter ad campaigns into DoubleClick for the next year. And they hated it." Turnover was high, but Friedman sensed a new and better possibility.

For the autistic worker, Friedman says, "It's nice to know that the next task looks like the last task." So he launched AutonomyWorks to take those repetitive tasks that needed flawless execution, yet were drudgery for most workers, and created a platform for employment for his son and others. The company built an entire business system to bring on board, train, and support autistic adults in roles performing back-office marketing operations, tapping into their attention to detail, and not just a willingness but preference for repetitive work.

"No one's ever done AutonomyWorks before," he says. "There is no model. There is no pattern what that's going to look like." Despite the unknowns, he had serious mission and motivation: "I couldn't live with myself knowing that I had an idea that could have changed the life for my son and I didn't do it."

Dave Friedman's story got bigger than just finding a job for his son. "Even if AutonomyWorks is hugely successful and we employ 10,000 people, in the next decade 500,000 people with autism are going to graduate out of school and enter the workforce," he says. "And that's just in the US."

His mission—his dream now—is to change the way the world views autism and inspire others to help tackle this pressing need. In a way he's a model for a new open-source movement where a successful organization is open to one and all to repeat, improve, and perfect. He can't do it all on his own, even if he sought to, and so will seed this to the world. If this is not an abundance-based form of leadership, what is?

TO IMAGINE AND REIMAGINE

While many Artists create from scratch, others are most innovative by bringing a new perspective to or reworking something that already exists. Chief Marketing Officer Joshua Katz loves to improve and perfect brands—their identity, message, and image. When he came on board VH1 television network, he noticed that adults over twenty-five had a completely different relationship with music. The phrase "Music First" revolutionized the channel and music industry.

From there he launched BBC America, then helped build the brand for the ABC Family (Freeform), where he observed a changing dynamic in American families that led to the tagline, "A New Kind of Family," which sustained the brand for the next five years.

Most recently Katz was tasked with reimagining a legacy brand, viewed by many as past its time. He took people's assumption that those over the age of sixty-five had no interest in social media and flipped it on its head. After he built a fan base of six million social media followers, the newly reinvigorated brand (we have been asked not to name it yet) now has a tribe who actively engage and view it as a sacred mission to promote it to others.

Like other great Artist leaders, Joshua Katz doubles down on his best abilities and continues to mold proverbial lumps of clay. He takes the stance that branding is never done. "The consumer is always teaching you something," he says. "So, you may have to rebuild it. You may have to remake it. You may have to reshape it. You may have to add to it."

Glen Tullman, CEO of three game-changing healthcare companies, notes that the current healthcare system is flawed because it incents all parties to spend more, not less. He said to us: "We need to envision something new and different in healthcare. Not better, because this current system, you can't make it better, it's fundamentally flawed and not aligned with the people who matter—all of us, our families and loved ones, and the businesses that employ us and along with us, pay the bills."

Tullman's most recent company, Livongo, completely re-envisioned care for people with diabetes, and then added hypertension, weight management, and behavioral health, serving a population of one million-plus before merging with Teladoc Health.

Now he's at it again with Transcarent, which aims to create a new kind of health and care experience, focused on quality of care and experience, not cost. Driven by data science that creates both understanding of an individual's needs and personalization, it equips people with information, guidance, and easy access and puts them back in charge of their care.

INNOVATING BACK TO THE FUTURE

In 2009, shovels hit the ground in Antakya, Turkey, to build a new luxury hotel. Then, surprise! As the site was being excavated, ruins from the ancient city of Antioch, once home to 200,000, were found right where the hotel would sit. It was as if 2,300 years had rolled away as ancient walls, columns, tile, marble sculptures, and beautiful mosaics emerged from the dirt and rubble.

So much for the original blueprint. All the plans were scrapped and the owners brought on an award-winning architect to rethink the possibilities, culminating in the Museum Hotel's debut ten years later in what the *Financial Times* describes as "surely the most remarkable hotel to launch anywhere in the world so far this year." Standing atop four acres of the ancient downtown, it exemplifies how two traditional concepts—hotel and museum—could be completely reimagined into a new experience.

The restaurant industry is another arena that attracts reinvention and fresh thinking, fertile ground for Artists and innovative leadership. "There are many Artist leaders—people who start a concept and grow it," says Shan Atkins. "They don't necessarily stay forever, but it's all about their vision and it really is art."

Atkins serves on the board of directors of Darden, a large full-service restaurant company with over 1,500 locations, 150,000 employees, and eight brands ranging from Olive Garden to Long-Horn Steakhouse. She explains that a lot goes into launching a new restaurant. All kinds of questions must be answered: Why does the new concept deserve to live when the world is full of restaurants? What's going to be unique about it? What about the guest experience, the environment, the menu? What kind of service will be delivered to the guest each and every time?

THE CRITIC'S LAMENT

Whether creating from scratch or reimagining and building on something already in the market, the critic's lament is that innovation is hard to do over and over again. Companies lose their creative mojo all the time, but for the innovative, the risk is in execution, timing, and market acceptance, not in the fertility of fresh ideas and solutions. Artist leaders know in their bones that the wellspring is infinite, no matter the industry, arena, place, or time.

With a track record of big ideas, the Artist could win the award for most envied of all leadership styles. There is this perception that innovators must be naturally gifted, perhaps endowed with creative powers the rest of us lack. So much of what comes from the Artist leader, however, is a result of tapping into what's going on around them and applying rigorous process, experience, trial and error, collaboration, and trust in oneself.

There is a fable about an emperor who tells his courtiers and advisers to bring him the most brilliant artist in the kingdom. The best artist is then presented to the emperor, who asks him to paint the greatest painting ever painted. The artist agrees, saying he will need twenty years to complete the masterpiece. The emperor grants his request and sends him on his way. Twenty years pass and the artist is again summoned. The emperor asks, "Where is the painting?" The artist calls for a blank canvas and paints the perfect painting—on the spot.

"You can't say you are going to have a zen-like supernova blast of an idea by a certain date," says Chief Information Officer Dean Samuels, who describes what he does as a technology executive to be both functional and relational. "I need to learn from the CEO, the management team, customers, and staff. I need to learn the business you are in, and the business you want to be in," he says.

He can build you the technology road map to get there, but it's the relationship building combined with functioning in the role that cause flashes of an idea. A spark of creativity. The path to business transformation that leads to unfair competitive advantage. As an on-demand CIO, while Samuels is drawn to helping midsize companies, he says massive companies have just as big a need for artistry. "If we spend a million and get a $10 million return because of a creative technology investment, that's my best day," he says.

THE POWER TO ACT

The Artist as organizational leader is both aspirational and pragmatic. "At the end of all this I want to be able to stand up and say that we created a successful, growing, profitable business," says Dave Friedman. While many people's creations end up unseen, or quashed by the fear of criticism or being an outlier, for real Artists, their creation must see the light of day.

"*Act* is my favorite word," says world-renowned artist Ai Weiwei. "Creativity is the power to act. It counts to take action; a small act is worth a million thoughts. That is the most important lesson of my life."

Shipping an idea out to the world is not a guarantee of success. All Artists fail. It is part of the fabric of creativity and innovation to fail repeatedly on the way to success and market acceptance.

James Dyson described the discovery process to the *New York Times*: "Almost everything you do is a failure, until you get the one success that works." It took five years of failing to figure out how to create a little cyclone inside his vacuum cleaners, finally leading to his first big product win. He has added to the Dyson portfolio with innovative or revolutionary washing machines, fans, heaters, air purifiers, hand dryers, and hair dryers.

"We're trying to go where nobody's gone before and you tend to get lost when you do," innovation guru Jeff Leitner told us. Find a way or make one, the need to create and pave a fresh path is in the Artist leader's DNA, and even if there was a clear path, the Artist wouldn't take it.

John DeLorean insisted on gull-wing doors on his car, damn the cost. Steve Jobs demanded the Next Cube computer feature true 90-degree angles, despite the huge added manufacturing and molding expense, because true right angles just looked more elegant. An 89-degree angle, just one teeny tiny degree off, could pop out of a standard mold, but that just wouldn't cut it for Jobs.

Elon Musk battled with the SEC because no one puts a muzzle on Elon. Warren Beatty had a stunning track record right up until he decided to produce and star in *Ishtar*, reckoned one of the worst movies ever made. Webvan ran through $1 billion in funding in the internet bubble with exactly zero to show for it. Chernobyl's engineers knew their nuclear reactor design was, at least in theory, so safe it didn't need a strong containment vessel. Then it blew up, contaminating surrounding lands, flora, and fauna for hundreds of miles.

Failure is part and parcel of experimentation, and experimentation is the soil in which the Artist plants many seeds, seeing what will grow, what must be culled, and what could bear fruit if nurtured and rejiggered just so. No Artist comes to greatness without face-planting again and again.

"I try to minimize the cost of risk, but I do not try to minimize risk ever," says Jeff Leitner. "I will launch anything I think is a great idea, and I will try to do it in a way that my start-up costs are not that high and that the cost of failure will not bankrupt me. But I don't hold off on launching it because it might fail."

What happens when an Artist hits a dead end? The beauty of their wiring is that they will create all over again. Michael Sonnenfeldt was a successful real estate developer and investor who led other ventures before creating TIGER 21, a premier membership organization catering to high-net-worth investors. "For me the most exciting driving force in my career has been being part of the act of creation," he says. "If TIGER 21 disappeared tomorrow, I'd be starting something else because that's where my mind naturally wanders."

THE NECESSITY OF PARALLEL TRACKS

This driving force also fuels a compulsion for many Artists to be engaged in numerous projects simultaneously. Mark Cuban started with Broadcast.com, but after the sale he expanded into ventures ranging from Magnolia Pictures to *Shark Tank* to the NBA's Dallas Mavericks. Jack Dorsey has Twitter and Square. Danny Meyer's Union Square Hospitality Group continues to invent winning restaurant creations in addition to Gramercy Tavern, winner of nine James Beard Awards, and the trendy and famous fast-food chain, Shake Shack.

To see if someone has Artist wiring, just look at whether they have a single focus or take on multiple, parallel projects. The Artist needs intentional distraction.

Dean Samuels serves up to three companies simultaneously as a technology executive, which has taken him around the world, from Paris to Beijing to Sao Paolo and across industries from telecom to healthcare to e-commerce. Samuels found that it wasn't as exciting when he was working with just one company and says that "something about volatility and the mixture of switching back and forth between functions, relationships, and entities stimulates creativity."

"I remember years back, a person told me that I needed to be solely dedicated to one company," he says. "My take is more the mercenary who has fought many wars and is still alive, still winning. You want to be in the foxhole with *that* guy."

The Artist Leader		
• Creative	• Multitasker	• Visionary
• Nonconformist	• Relentless	• Outsider
• Self-reliant	• Resilient	• Disrupter
• Revolutionary	• Renegade	• Aspirational

In the Trenches with Artists

"We're trying to go where nobody's gone before and you tend to get lost when you do. It's like saying, how come Lewis and Clark took so many wrong paths? Why couldn't they have been more like somebody else? And the answer was because they were trying to figure out something that nobody else had figured out."
—Jeff Leitner

Artists fight conformity. How can they be effective if their starting position is "against" the world?

This section is a deeper dive into Artists' winning habits. These are not parallel habits to, say, the Fixer's toolkit. For the Fixer there is a linear process with specific systems and approaches designed to increase the chances of successfully saving an organization. For the Artist, the challenge is how to travel the long road, from idea, to innovation, to widespread adoption. The Artist's supreme challenge is how to get the spark out of their heads, past the gauntlet of team, colleagues, bosses, and boards and into manifested reality, into the minds, hearts, and pockets of their audience, tribe, stakeholders, and consumers.

Artists well know that people think they are crazy. And they might agree. The critics may be temporarily silenced when the work of innovation—the new and different—finally clicks and finds its market. The road to get there, however, is usually a battle. It's easy to absorb the message to persist when you are getting positive feedback. Praise. Sales. Kudos. Market share. Awards. Likes and retweets.

But for the innovator out on the edge, it's a vacuum, which is what makes this leadership mode so hard. For the Artist, attention is gold. The opposite—to be ignored—can seem like death.

In the late 1800s, French Impressionist painter Claude Monet's canvases of blurry images made no sense. Even among fellow artists, contemporaries must have thought he was nuts. "I am distressed, almost discouraged, and fatigued to the point of feeling slightly ill," Monet wrote to a friend. "What I am doing is no good, and in spite of your confidence, I am very much afraid that my efforts will all lead to nothing."

Lucky for us, Monet didn't quit. He hit haystacks no less than twenty-five times, Notre Dame thirty times, and water lilies 250 times. And those are just the surviving works of genius. Who knows how many he tossed.

When Robert Louis Stevenson committed to being a writer, his father told him, "You have rendered my whole life a failure." Despite his father's view of his failure, luckily Stevenson kept plugging away, giving the world *Treasure Island*, *Kidnapped*, and *The Strange Case of Dr. Jekyll and Mr. Hyde*.

Innovation guru and author Jeff Leitner says, "It is pathological more than part and parcel, meaning it is a part of our unique psychological makeup that we tolerate failure." The discipline is in facing the page every day to write.

FIGHT THE RESISTANCE, ENGAGE THE TEAM

The Fixer's secret sauce is in the doing, and the more practiced they become, the more techniques at their disposal. For the Artist, the secret sauce is in how to fight the resistance, as author Stephen Pressfield puts it in his wonderful manifesto, *The War of Art*. Successful Artist leaders have developed tools and techniques to increase their chances of success.

The first hurdle for the Artist is to get out of their own head. To be able to listen to the customer (even if for no other reason than to reject what is conventional). Before launching Airbnb, Brian Chesky worked on designing children's ventilators. He had to put himself in the patient's mind to design with empathy. In an interview with LinkedIn founder Reid Hoffman, he recalled that at Airbnb he had to relearn the lesson.

Early on, the company had very few customers. An investor gave him the nudge he needed, telling Chesky in California to get on a plane bound for New York, go to his few customers, and get to know them. He says the insights from these visits formed the backbone of what the company stands for today.

Chief Marketing Officer Whitney Vosburgh has built brands at three global companies, so when healthcare behemoth McKesson asked Vosburgh to help increase franchisee sign-ups and products delivered at one of their holdings—Health Mart, the fifth largest pharmacy chain in America—he jumped at the opportunity. He saw a much bigger possibility for Health Mart. Vosburgh discovered that most of the pharmacies were scattered throughout rural, small-town America and owned and operated by multigenerational families.

"It's the family business and they've been in the communities for a long time," he says, painting a picture of old soda fountains or potbelly stoves where customers come in to warm their hands and enjoy a coffee or hot cocoa.

Vosburgh continued to look for what makes this different, and what makes it tick. He had a breakthrough. "The community was involved and celebrated their caregivers, the people who made sure their elders and their loved ones got the right meds, the right way, at the right time. And it celebrated the pharmacists and the pharmacies as their hubs of community care," he says.

This insight led to a complete repositioning of Health Mart and the local family pharmacies and pharmacists as champions of community care. The advertising and branding campaign that followed produced results ten times greater than expectations. Management said to Vosburgh: "We would have been delighted with a 30 percent increase in new franchisee sign-ups, but you in less than six months have increased it by over 300 percent as well as adding one and a half billion dollars' worth of revenue."

His voracious appetite for "doing new things, and old things in new ways" was inspired during his days in training at Parsons School of Design where his favorite professor told him to do something new every day. "Even if you're right-handed, brush your teeth with your left hand," Vosburgh says. "It's all about neuroplasticity, of developing new learning paths in your mind and then into your life."

In order for a product or service to see the light of day, the Artist leader must engage the team, avoiding the temptation to try and do everything themselves as the originator of the idea. AutonomyWorks CEO Dave Friedman pushes curiosity down to the team, telling them, "Let's not just be like everybody else. Let's find out where the white space is, what are people not doing, what's the different unique combination of creative and data and business technology that will actually create a different kind of company."

THE ART OF DISTRACTION

It is a truism to say that focus is good and distraction is bad, yet Artists need distraction and diversion. Most innovators paint on multiple canvases at the same time. It is like oxygen for the Artist to have an occasional pressure release to the task at hand. The Artist dives deep into an ocean of discovery, exploration, learning, and wondering, and in the midst of insights and bursts of creativity, they occasionally come up for air. That shift to surfacing from the deep before diving back down is a necessary and purposeful shift in attention from one project to another, with the ultimate goal of finishing the main project. The roadblocks to creative conclusion tend to get worked out by alternatives along the way.

For some Artists, the outlet might be multiple companies, and for others it might be another passion. "I spend 30 percent of my time focused on things that never make me a dime but have made me very happy trying to figure out whether I can create something and bring it to life," explains Chief Marketing Officer Joshua Katz. "I do my own stuff, whether it's writing a screenplay, coming up with an idea for a website, helping a start-up that isn't paying me, but fulfills me. Whatever it happens to be, I need that to nourish me."

Former *Tonight Show* host Jay Leno credits his love of tinkering with his 187 cars and 163 motorcycles in tandem with his ability to keep taking his comedy act on the road, coming up with killer jokes and shtick 200 nights a year. In an interview in the *Wall Street Journal*, he said, "I work in a business that's subjective. Some people think you suck, and some people think you're great. The problem is, they're both correct. But it's different with a car: when you take something that's broken and you make it run, no one can say you didn't fix it. I work at night in my head trying to say things, and in the day I work putting things together. It's a nice sense of balance."

David Ormesher says, "The need for multiple canvases resonates very deeply with me." When he is not in Rwanda helping Bigger Future, he is leading his 175-person marketing services firm, while also serving as Chairman of the Board at the Lyric Opera of Chicago (along with other nonprofit roles). To him the nonprofits are "as important to life as my day jobs" and still give him the leeway for relentless focus and extreme sacrifice in growing and reinventing his company over and over.

And just when you think your Artist's plate is full, check again. Richard Scherrer, the engineer listed first on the patent for Lockheed's F-117 Nighthawk stealth aircraft, worked at NASA, then Lockheed, then Northrop, followed by stints at DARPA, Boeing, and Sikorsky. He was responsible for groundbreaking design, test, and production on dozens of advanced aircraft. And yet, he had a side hustle, long before the term *gig economy* came around. In his spare time, Scherrer did work for Walt Disney, designing rides for the Disneyland theme park including Matterhorn, Dumbo, Tea Party, Little Train that Could, and Flying Saucers.

While leading a full suite of IT functions for multiple companies, Dean Samuels found that another creative outlet was essential. For him it's music. "I was a software engineer and played at a piano bar six days a week," Samuels recalls of his early career. Today he jams on his jazz piano and Hammond organ. While music is different from technology leadership, he finds the creative process to be similar. If you took away his ability to work with multiple clients and in other channels, he says he would "lose passion, creativity, compassion, stimulation, and ideas that come out of nowhere unplanned."

LAUNCHING A THOUGHT EXPERIMENT

Artists have a greater chance of success by taking leaps, not baby steps. The bigger the vision, the more chance of enlisting and enrolling the team. David Ormesher began his biggest leap in digital marketing with a thought experiment. He asked himself: Would a big company in New York ever hire us? His answer was no. While they had a good reputation and plenty of clients, there wasn't any particular reason a big company would look at them twice.

Ormesher's solution was gut wrenching. His marketing services company, closerlook, inc., had to focus more if it was going to stand out. He decided to zero in on just three industries and forgo everything else. And it worked, for a while. They experienced national growth and scored new clients. But after a couple years, Ormesher realized he still couldn't truly claim deep expertise in any of their clients' industries. It wasn't enough.

Looking at the range of markets and customers their clients served, he went to his team with an announcement. "We are going to focus on digital marketing . . . in only one area," he remembers, creating a little uncomfortable stir in the room. He set out a plan to put all their eggs in one basket: pharmaceutical marketing.

"It meant firing clients that were multimillion-dollar accounts. Major brands that everybody knows that we had been working with for years, but weren't in pharma or healthcare," he recalls. Over the next six months he said goodbye to clients who no longer fit the new focus. While the process was painful, Ormesher was convinced that being a generalist was good, but not great, and his goal was to be best in the world.

The team spent about twelve months holding their breath to see how the decision would turn out.

He could tell about halfway through that long year that they had made the right decision: "As if the universe was sort of conspiring with us, the pharma industry responded and within another six months after we had fired all of our previous clients, we were able to backfill enough new revenue to replace what we lost from firing clients." The bet paid off. "Our growth rate went to 40 percent. The trajectory went like a hockey stick," says Ormesher.

The effect on the team was just as profound. "Building deep expertise and capabilities enabled a level of confidence starting with me and then throughout the firm to be able to stand up and say we do this, we know this, we're the best," he says. "That level of confidence and authenticity, for everybody to get up in the morning and look themselves in the mirror and say 'I know what I stand for'—that's priceless."

Picasso said, "Art is the elimination of the unnecessary." Ormesher's bold work is a hallmark of the Artist, but he says that only by focusing and then refocusing did everything else become simple.

"You know who your customers are. It's now a finite set. You know who your employees should be and what capabilities to hire around. Employees know if they're going to grow as professionals, where to study and what to focus on," he says. He noticed an even bigger benefit for his clients: "You see the same problems over and over again and begin to use pattern recognition to allow you to identify, diagnose, and come up with solutions much faster and much more cost effectively."

THE UNGOVERNED CREATION

The Artist leader driving to excess can simultaneously produce greatness and seeming ungovernability. Is it an Icarus moment, flying too close to the sun?

Theranos was a Silicon Valley unicorn. In 2003, founder Elizabeth Holmes dropped out of Stanford at age nineteen to start the business. With a revolutionary technology that allowed drug stores to have mini walk-in clinics where patients could get results of blood tests on demand, the company raised over $900 million from investors.

Questions emerged about the effectiveness of the technology and reliability of critically important test results. Nonetheless, Holmes and team pressed forward with expansion plans and new product rollouts, ballooning to a $9 billion valuation by 2014. A year later it all started to derail, as more and more allegations of faulty technology arose culminating with an SEC investigation and charges of massive fraud. What was once celebrated as breakthrough innovation had stretched too far.

And yet most corporations come nowhere close to excess and extravagant creativity, let alone any type of boldness or risk taking. The failure of much of the corporate world to innovate and instead copy or play it safe speaks volumes for lack of paying attention to their Artist leaders within. It is easy to conflate Artist with rugged, individualistic entrepreneur, but we don't think that's valid. Many innovators and wild thinkers choose corporate confines. Unfortunately, much of what could be bold leaps by established players are quashed by unimaginative, timid managers kowtowing to the short-term tyranny of shareholders who demand share buybacks and dividends at all costs.

How to view decisions by IBM, Intel, Cisco, and Oracle that systematically bought back their own shares over the past two decades, reducing their outstanding share count by 40% to 50%? They are not alone, and, yes, they propped up their share prices, but it begs the question: What *would* have happened had they more aggressively pursued new markets and bold leaps, instead of, as a *Financial Times* writer put it, engaged in "slowly devouring themselves"?

Matt Ridley wrote in his book, *How Innovation Works: And Why It Flourishes in Freedom*, "Throughout the economy, with the exception of the digital industry, the West is experiencing an innovation famine. The Austrian economist Joseph Schumpeter's 'perennial gale of creative destruction' has been replaced by the gentle breezes of rent-seeking."

The need for expert Artist leaders is essential for forward progress and breakthrough innovation. The Artist is the driving force needed to renew an organization that loses purpose, loses its market leading position, sees competitors leaping ahead with bolder ideas, or is in need of sources of fresh growth. From the invention of messenger RNA-based vaccines to blockchain, and even privatized space travel, Artists are the out-at-the-edge, way off from the center of things foundation from which discontinuous leaps occur and great improvements take place.

You Know You Are an Artist If . . .

✓ You are driven to create.

✓ You envision, re-envision, or reinvent, whether its ideas, products, services, brands, messages.

✓ You view anything traditional or a norm as having a target on its back.

✓ You bring others along by tapping into and mobilizing deeper values, motivations, and shared purpose.

✓ You can be seen as or may feel like an outsider.

✓ You appreciate the bureaucrats, as long as they leave you alone.

✓ You have multiple initiatives going on simultaneously.

✓ You challenge the status quo.

✓ Your superpower is turning your evergreen curiosity into innovation.

✓ You value fresh thinking, especially your own take.

✓ You know the creative wellspring never runs dry.

✓ You view everything as an experiment.

✓ You are in heaven when they are paying attention, relieved when product ships.

✓ You draw inspiration from, well, everything and anything.

✓ You see failure as a stepping-stone to discovery and breakthrough.

3.
THE BUILDER

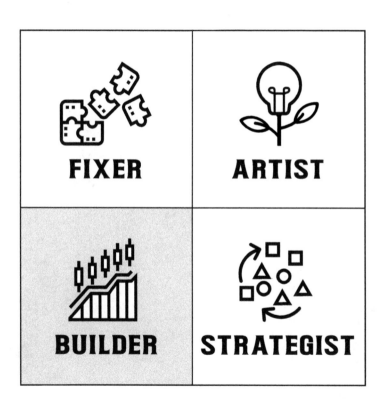

FIXER

ARTIST

BUILDER

STRATEGIST

A Builder Story:
If You Build a Temple,
Will It IPO?

You might get flashbacks to your own childhood hearing Russ Reeder talk about growing up building go-karts and treehouses or starting up a lawn mowing business to make some extra cash. But his upbringing was anything but ordinary.

He was a child of divorced parents, and Russ's father would come to pick up Russ and his sister and take them to spend the weekends with his grandfather who lived and taught leadership at West Point, the United States Military Academy.

His grandfather, Colonel Russell Potter "Red" Reeder Jr., was a decorated US Army commander and creator of the Bronze Star Medal. On June 6, 1944, he led 3,200 men from the 12th Infantry Regiment who landed on Utah Beach, one of the five sectors where Allied troops landed in the Normandy region of France on D-day.

As Allied forces pushed inland against fierce German resistance, Colonel Reeder faced a big dilemma. His soldiers had been dropped on a stretch of coastline two miles off course from the planned landing zone. The senior general in overall command of Utah Beach ordered Colonel Reeder to hike his troops along the shore to the point where they were supposed to have landed, but as he looked out at his men, under intense fire with casualties piling up all around, he told the commander "absolutely not." Instead, they pressed forward and inland, slogging through swamps and flooded marshes to get to the rendezvous point.

With that kind of family legacy, Russ Reeder says it was instilled in him at a young age that "it was expected that you take care of people, and you take care of your team—you would think it's the normal way to do things."

Talk of his grandfather's best friend, President Eisenhower, or of his grandfather's mentoring of future greats like Vince Lombardi—who would later take the Green Bay Packers to five NFL championships—were regular occurrences around the dinner table. While at West Point, the colonel published over thirty-five books about leadership, history, and sports and even played baseball for the Giants for a short time before returning to the military.

"I was lucky enough to have such a domineering coach and grandfather," the younger Reeder says, adding that his grandfather was stern, but kind. It was his grandfather, ultimately, who set a foundation for his grandson to take on future leadership roles.

BUILDERS BREAK THROUGH CEILINGS

Today Russ Reeder is a master at leading organizations and teams seeking to bust through seemingly unbreakable ceilings. "I've seen businesses that are successful at $20 million in revenue, or $60 million, or over $100 million, and they just hit this barrier," he says. "What got them to that position won't get them to where they want to go next."

Too often organizations envision more revenue, expanded product, an organized and aligned team, but they stall. They just can't get to the next level. It's this unique challenge that energizes Reeder—a Builder leader—who over the past twenty years has led eight companies ranging from $20 million to $3 billion in revenue. In every case there was one thing in common: a laser focus on growth.

His greatest victory so far is Media Temple, a web hosting company that already had steady revenues, thousands of customers, and a solid brand. A challenge remained though. No longer a young start-up, the company hadn't reached a dominant or unassailable position. Instead, it was in a state of limbo. If they were to continue growing, they needed to find more profitable solutions in a world pushing hard to commoditize their services.

The company also had a strange dynamic—two founders each with a very different vision for the future. One no longer wanted to work in the business or pursue anything new or creative in product or branding. The other wanted to zero in on operations and grow the business. The tension between the two would prove to be a major challenge itself, never mind its implications for the company.

Reeder parachuted in and took the role of President, knowing that in addition to running day-to-day operations, he would become "almost like the counselor between the two founders" who were in a constant state of flipping between selling the business, buying out one of the partners, or continuing to expand.

He immersed himself in the team and culture, committing himself to "be a sponge and consume what's working, what's not, and what they wanted to do." He saw that while Media Temple's products were good, bigger issues were brewing. The competitive landscape was about to explode.

Amazon Web Services (AWS) was on the march and had Media Temple's market within its sights. They had arrived on the scene, seemingly out of nowhere. Amazon deciding to sell against you would be a death sentence for most companies, but Reeder wanted to approach the problem pragmatically.

He had noticed Media Temple's real claim to fame was white-glove customer support. They couldn't ignore or fight Amazon head-on, so it was far better to double down on their core strength and, even more to the point, use competitors like Amazon to reinforce their own offering.

Rather than wait for customers to hit the exit, he launched a partnership program where Media Temple gave customers the tools to take full advantage of AWS. But he didn't stop there. Instead, he kept adding on more would-be competitors like Google Compute Engine.

It proved to be a winning combination. The company went on a tear, with revenues doubling in three years. And as the new services got going, an even bigger opportunity presented itself. Domain registrar and website services company GoDaddy had been looking for a premium offering, and Media Temple was just the ticket.

With $3 billion in revenue, and close to 4,000 employees, GoDaddy acquiring Media Temple was a huge victory. It didn't prove to be an easy marriage, however. "GoDaddy at the time was struggling with their brand identity," Reeder says. "The founder was shooting elephants and having women in bikinis on TV commercials and just had an offensive brand."

Reeder and his team anticipated upset customers when the deal was announced, and, sure enough, word on the street was that Media Temple had sold out. What once was a company with great products and a great brand was now supposedly ruined.

"We were trending on Twitter for three days when we announced the acquisition," Reeder says. "We had planned for this chaos. Media Temple was number one trending on Twitter, GoDaddy was second, and 'turn back on the US government' was third. We had a 24/7 response team, sixteen people in the room on social media for three days, twenty-four hours a day."

He compares the crisis to the idea of, say, Walmart buying Nordstrom. "There would be huge issues on both ends," says Reeder. "Customers of Nordstrom would never shop there again—the true Nordstrom lovers. And then the people of Walmart are going to ask, 'Why are you buying that company?'"

The deal ultimately survived with GoDaddy acquiring Media Temple for its strengths in technology, customer support process, products, and growing customer base. After the merger was completed, GoDaddy asked Reeder to stay on to help the newly enlarged company kick into a higher gear. Ensconced as one of the top executives at GoDaddy, he led the charge in implementing a new mission, vision, and values across the organization, creating a management training program on better leadership practices for over 600 of the top executives, and preparing for a blockbuster IPO.

Going public brought a wave of excitement, but Reeder began to feel that he could add more value elsewhere. "I had this great management team, and I was not going to replace the CEO of GoDaddy anytime soon," he recalls. Despite the public gloss, after GoDaddy acquired Media Temple, they decided to utilize their technology and web hosting capabilities but didn't focus on melding the two companies together. Once GoDaddy rolled out a higher-end offering, the divisions were left essentially competing against one another for customers.

Reeder defines his role as needing to understand the details of the business, while being clear that his job is to work *on* the business, not *in* the business. That means focusing "on the processes and procedures to make your employees successful." In addition, he wants to make sure the tools are there to do more with less rather than less with more. He jokes that his wife tells him he is a little bit of a control freak: "I like to make sure things are in their place . . . and ensure things are done right versus just done fast."

That attention to detail has propelled him to becoming expert at putting structure in place, but once something feels like it's moving into day-to-day maintenance mode, it's time for him to move on.

After his stint at GoDaddy, Russ Reeder gave his next build a go, this time jumping in to help expand the largest web hosting business in Europe by bringing them to the US, in the form of a new stand-alone company, OVHcloud US.

Within two years the US division went from zero revenue and zero employees to close to $100 million. How does a Builder seemingly go from win to win? He reflects, "To me the definition of luck is the harder you work the luckier you get."

What happened next could only be described as a very lucky break on top of something that was already remarkable. VMware happened to be looking to divest their cloud division, and in a competitive bidding process OVH beat out IBM. Reeder's company went into turbocharged growth mode, inheriting 225 employees and over 1,000 customers.

This presented a new set of challenges integrating cultures and systems. He and his team went to work implementing new financial, customer support, and HR systems and built two new data centers to integrate into the parent company's global armada of twenty-seven data centers—all bread-and-butter activities for market-climbing leaders.

THE BUILDING OF A BUILDER

The journey to becoming a master organization Builder was not exactly predictable for Reeder. Though he attended West Point Prep, a military-style prep school that would have had him follow in his grandpa's footsteps, Reeder decided that the family military tradition was not for him. It was a difficult conversation, especially after his grandfather landed in the hospital with stomach problems the day after Reeder broke the news.

"I wanted to do more business, computers, and software engineering than I would have been able to do in the military," he says, adding that serving five years in the military to then come out and compete for a job in a quickly evolving technology landscape seemed like a long time to not be doing what he loved. "I like change faster. In the military, it takes longer by design, to implement change and see results. So the way I looked at it was that I needed to be in an entrepreneurial, high-pressure setting that would like to see change and enjoyed a culture of change."

Reeder kicked off his career in the tech world, quickly making the jump from a software programmer to sales engineering and into sales and sales management within the applications business at Oracle, where he saw the division skyrocket from $300 million to $3 billion in sales. He then moved to a software start-up backed by leading venture capital firm Sequoia, which had its own high-pressure mindset.

He was hooked. There was an unmistakable energy in high-growth environments. And he had a knack for picking winners. He developed a playbook that started with a checklist to gauge whether he should drop into an opportunity. Whether it was taking on a CEO role in an investor-backed company or serving alongside the founder, he looks at the same three criteria:

- First, he asks: **Is there a large and growing market?** What problem are they trying to solve, where is the market, and is there a there, there? Even the best master plans, procedures, and team will fall flat without clarity and a large addressable market.

- Next, he asks: **How good is the product, and does it have traction?** Not only does there need to be an opportunity to make the product better, but he looks for enough of a base where he can turn customers into evangelists.
- Finally, he looks at the **people**—from employees to the board of directors, investors, and other decision-makers. "Coming in as the CEO, you can start to change the culture and start to replace the people, but you can't drop into a toxic culture and change everything," he says.

Reeder believes that with the combination of market, product, and people you can do amazing things. And his formula has worked. In helping company after company work to dominate a market, he says, "Never once did I go in specifically just trying to sell the business. Instead, the main goal was to grow." Yet, there is a pattern. Almost every business he has taken on—from software to digital publishing to security and data retention in the cloud—either led to an IPO or successful sale.

"Everything you do is a bet," says Reeder, who is a fan of hockey legend Wayne Gretzky's line about skating to where the puck is going to be. But it's even harder in the unbounded game of business, especially in technology products where innovators leapfrog each other seemingly daily. He says, "It's not only making your bet on where you want the company to be and where you want the product to be, but you have to understand where the market is going to be."

Making predictions about people, markets, and the future may be futile, but if you want one very sharp-line definition of the difference between a manager and a leader, Reeder has hit it squarely: managers can't and won't predict, leaders will and do. His batting average is pretty darn good by anyone's reckoning, but Reeder would be the first to say he's had misses.

After he left GoDaddy, he was recruited to an early-stage company focused on civic engagement. It was a worthy mission, but it turned out to be a bust. They weren't first to market and the competition had more funding. Even worse, a toxic culture developed as the founders and board fought nonstop, putting the management team in the midst of the drama. "When the facts change, you have to be nimble and change your plan," Reeder says, ultimately deciding to pull the plug on his involvement.

He has learned when to call it quits. "Failing is very humbling. I can point out failures in every one of my deals and what lessons I've learned from each one." Having worked in software and cloud application companies attempting to dominate fast-growing markets, he sees his worst day as when you fail the customer, giving an example of a system going down where the customer loses access to their data— or worse, the client's customers' systems go down.

He ensures procedures are in place to avoid customer outages at all costs. Whether it's an act of Mother Nature or, for some other reason, multiple redundant systems fail, there are plans to get back up and running as soon as possible. You can tell this is core to who Reeder is: when things go wrong, being responsive, honest, and transparent with customers is mandatory if you're going to regain their trust. "You always find out what people are made of when you go through these really difficult situations," he says. There is humility in this, and a steely resolve to keep moving forward.

LESSONS FROM GRANDFATHER

One of his grandfather's lessons keeps coming back to Reeder: leadership matters. "It's the butterfly effect," he says. "You can positively affect people, then they positively affect others, and then those people far beyond you affect still more people in a positive way."

Inspiring leadership can be a force multiplier beyond easy understanding. For example, a bad leader might yell at employees or put them in stressful situations, and then that employee goes home and yells at their spouse or kids and puts them in stressful situations.

"You can really change people's lives," Reeder says. "Too many leaders let mission get in the way of simple responsibility." It is a lesson often lost on organizations stuck in day-to-day minutiae or caught up in labyrinthine systems or enthralled in the power of technology. He has seen many companies get distracted: "It's that shiny object syndrome. They start all these projects, but it's not toward one mission, it's not toward one product road map."

He knows he is wired as a product-driven CEO, ensuring the problem being solved is clearly defined, then creating a product road map and timeline that will guide everyone from engineering to marketing, customer support, and lead generation.

Russ Reeder moves the team into an agile, quick-win mindset where people aren't working on side projects that someone spins up just because they thought a customer would want it. "It is critical to create an environment that fuels innovation while adhering to a pragmatic product road map built from real customer use cases and market needs," he says, adding that it can be incredibly frustrating for the team to work on a project that never goes into production.

He believes that companies really start to get in trouble—really start to go by the wayside—when they move into maintenance mode and lack the thrust and internal propulsion to stay ahead. "Companies die from within," says Reeder who emphasizes that if you are not growing, you're dying, a mark of a Builder who will avoid stasis at all costs to go after ceiling-busting market domination. It's winner take all.

The Builder Leadership Mode

Market is mantra for the Builder.

The Builder leader sees the gaps, the opportunities, and the dangers within an organization, likewise focusing on customer needs, problems, and aspirations. By storm, by fire, by clever or blunt force, organically or by acquisition, by carving out what exists or making an entirely new market or industry, the Builder will grow or be damned. The Builder is our icebreaker, charging forward, ever onward.

This leader is the linchpin in the evolution of a business. Whether moving from a product or widget into a stand-alone company, division, or platform, or looking to expand into new markets or verticals, the Builder ensures an organization is in a strong position to run at scale. Systems and processes are put in place, a team is built out and strengthened, and a bigger strategy drives expansion.

"It started when I was in retail at twenty-three, but I like to hear the register ring. I love to see revenue grow," says beauty, fashion, and retail executive Lisa Yarnell. She found she had a knack for taking neglected product lines or business units within larger organizations from Colgate to L'Oréal and turning them into opportunity.

"It's about expanding product, category, customer base, geography, need fulfillment. There's just a hundred different ways we could get there," she says, "and it really takes somebody from outside to do those things."

Jaime Ellertson has led five consecutive software companies, growing each to the point of significant sale or IPO. He has seen founders and teams spend years trying to achieve sales, then often grow tired or lose perspective, not being able to see the forest for the trees.

"There is a period where people get to $10, $15, or $20 million with the business and they have reached their capacity to build the company and grow it," he says. Ellertson steps into an organization at a pivotal point to infuse new thinking, process, plans, and team—and get to a much higher level of orbit. There could have been a prior team or founder who maxed out in capability, whether operational, or financial or in market savvy.

His latest win, Everbridge, began as a collection of small software companies that provide critical event management for everything from public safety threats to IT outages to cyberattacks. In short order, the company came to dominate a multibillion-dollar industry that only came to size in the past decade or so. Under Ellertson's watch, Everbridge grew to 800 employees serving 4,500 corporate customers.

When assessing whether to invest time launching or joining a company, Ellertson first asks, "Are the markets large enough to sustain a real viable leader—and continue to grow?" Answering that question with a resounding yes is key for all successful Builders. The bigger drive, however, is not just opportunity for growth. It's desire, drive, thirst, and ambition for market domination.

THE BATTLE ROYALE FOR MARKET DOMINATION

Look under the covers of any thriving industry, and odds on there was a battle royale at the heart of it, with at least one bloody but triumphant Builder. Let's consider window cleaner sprays. Windex and Formula 409 are at the top of a now global market, but how did the market come to be dominated by just a few well-known and trusted products? In the case of Formula 409, credit one brilliant Builder, Wilson Harrell.

Harrell was not the inventor or company founder. He bought the company in the mid-1960s for $30,000 along with a famous television personality, Art Linkletter. Their goal was to take the product national. Unfortunately for them, in the midst of making ambitious plans, they landed on the radar of the 800-pound gorilla in consumer markets: Procter & Gamble. But Harrell kept his ear to the ground and heard some priceless gossip. He learned that P&G planned to launch a competitive product called Cinch by first testing it in three markets.

Harrell then made some bold moves. He decided to *withdraw* Formula 409 from those three markets. Remove all of it from store shelves. He went quiet, running silent and deep on purpose to mess with P&G's test. The Cincinnati giant launched its test, scoring predictably strong sales without much competition. Buoyed by its good results, P&G turned its attention to an even bigger rollout, not realizing that Harrell was effectively if not quite literally listening in on their plans and conversations.

He began his counterstrike behind the scenes.

Extra-large-sized spray containers rolled off Formula 409's production lines. Truckloads of coupons were printed and distributed, offering massive discounts. Store shelves were stocked with extra-large containers at reduced prices in stores throughout P&G's target cities. Harrell ensured that consumers would have squeaky clean windows for years and would not need to buy another window cleaning product for a long, long time.

When P&G finally debuted its product, it was a bust for the behemoth. As Harrell would tell audiences years later, he had a chance encounter with P&G's CEO after the launch. As Harrell laid on the praise extra thick, the CEO's only response was, "Oh, you. I've heard of you."

Major consumer products companies, including P&G, later courted Harrell, Linkletter, and partners who ultimately and successfully sold Formula 409 to Clorox.

Legendary Chicago hot-dog seller Dick Portillo also had market domination on the brain. Portillo founded a booming chain of forty restaurants called Portillo's sporting Chicago-style hot dogs, burgers, and a world-famous chocolate cake shake (Yes, as it sounds, a ginormous piece of chocolate cake tossed in a blender with vanilla ice cream. Amazing.).

In his autobiography, Portillo recalls Chicago Bears head coach Mike Ditka attempting to compete with his restaurants by launching Ditka Dogs. When Ditka's team raided a nearby Portillo's restaurant for talent, the move didn't sit well with Dick Portillo. He responded by asking a manager who had left to come back, offering the renegade manager $12,000 in cash. There were two conditions: he had to pull his workers back to Portillo's as well, and they had to walk away from Ditka's right before the grand opening. The result was chaos on the Ditka restaurant's opening, with missed orders, and inexperienced investors and managers scrambling to serve pissed off customers.

The Builder's desire to dominate can be found in every market, industry, stage, and sector. Michael Rubin sold his company, GSI Commerce, to eBay in 2011 for $2.4 billion. That was just his opening act, moving on to ramp up growth at three e-commerce sites: Rue La La, ShopRunner, and Fanatics.

In 2021 online sports merchandiser Fanatics acquired exclusive rights to trading cards for Major League Baseball and Major League Baseball Players Association, blindsiding the baseball trading card titan Topps, unlocking a seventy-year-long iron grip with the MLB. To top it all off, Fanatics simultaneously announced similar deals with the National Basketball Association, NBA players' unions, and the National Football League. Sheer genius.

SHOW ME THE MONEY

A successful Builder can be an investor's best friend, bridging the gap when expectations diverge between owners and operators. "The operating company is concerned about growth, and customers, and market awareness. Private equity is concerned about cash dropping to the bottom line. They are much less concerned about how those financial circumstances arrive," says Lisa Yarnell, who notes that for established companies there is usually a timeline to point of exit, which is a function of the tolerance of the investors.

Builders have an intense focus on their product, and it had better be good. "A flawed product either from inception that doesn't scale, doesn't deliver value, or isn't easy to use doesn't work in the model you're trying to deliver value in," Jaime Ellertson says. "If we're joining a company and trying to grow it, we want the product to be a working product or to have known issues that are correctable."

In equal measure for many Builders, they'll use acquisitions to get where they need to go. Ken Hunt acquired a small company that had a digital security product called Digipass. From a humble start he came to acquire sixteen companies, employ 700 people, and preside over a public company now known as OneSpan, generating $200 million revenue per year while serving 10,000 corporations and banks worldwide.

"We know our customers very, very well," he says, adding that "once we identify the kind of new product or new functionality they need, we would either build it ourselves or buy it through acquisition of a company."

CEO Lisa Yarnell found all kinds of consumer products that were unexploited gold mines at Colgate, L'Oréal, and other consumer companies. "There were products that nobody wanted to run, which I did." Maybe a product didn't geographically fit with what a company was doing, or the product category required an ingredient that was made in a factory someplace else. Whatever the background, Yarnell saw opportunity in brands that are very niche and highly profitable.

"I like to put a big magnifying glass on it," she says, asking the team what they would do if they didn't have the other 85 or 90 percent of the business to run. What once may have been viewed by people as the "place you go to die, or place you got moved when you didn't get promoted," now becomes the center of attention. This has become a Builder strength for Yarnell who says, "I make what I'm doing important to other people."

Michael Sonnenfeldt, who built multiple billion-dollar businesses, describes the aha moment when he got to the heart of his true leadership mode. Sonnenfeldt was meeting with an executive peer group to go over the results of personality assessments each had taken. The facilitator said, "There's somebody in the group who just loves creating things from nothing. He's an out-of-the-box thinker. He'll come up with things that nobody will think about."

Sonnenfeldt got ready to stand up, just as they announced his friend's name. "What the hell. I thought that was me," he recalls thinking. But his description came next: "This is not as much the out-of-the-box thinker as it is the weaver of other people's ideas and concepts into something that no one else could have woven to create an outcome." It was a profound distinction that Sonnenfeldt says he would not have understood until being confronted with it.

Whether early on, later stage, or part of a larger organization, the Builder transforms the elements to aggressively win over a market.

PRODUCT. PEOPLE. PROCESS.

Charlie Shalvoy has a track record of growing engineering and technology companies to the point of IPO or sale, repeatedly. His key to success? Like Jaime Ellertson and Russ Reeder, his focus is on product, people, and process. A sound product is key, and as for people, Shalvoy says having the *right* people in the *right* roles, at the *right* stage of a company's development is key to building a company.

"In certain stages of a company's size, one set of skills and experiences may be perfectly adequate," he says and gives the example of scaling a company to $50 million. "But then to go from $50 million to $200 million requires a much different set of skills, and from $200 million to a billion another set again. And there are some people that are able to add to their skill sets and grow with a company through different stages. Some cannot."

Builders are skilled at identifying good talent for the specific needs and stage of a company, multiplying themselves and their abilities in the process. Expert technology leader Griffin Caprio evolved from leading just a few programmers to running software development with hundreds of coders.

He describes his growth this way: "Creation and problem solving always underpinned where I came from in software development. As I began to get more experience, I realized that that same mentality exists at the people level as well. I realized I could multiply myself much larger by working through people and helping them as opposed to needing to do everything myself. It sounds cliché, but transitioning from focusing purely on the bits and bytes into focusing on the people allowed me to have a much greater impact than I would as a singular individual contributor."

"I think it starts with the people," says Lisa Yarnell. "If you have an organization that has high turnover, I promise you, nobody says thank you in it. And if you say thank you, . . . if you say, 'you did a good job' to people in an organization, they will work all day and night to make you successful."

Like many good Builders, Yarnell prides herself on making people feel good about their jobs and overall contribution, saying that when people feel good about what they do, they do it better and are more interested in helping you. "I want to make successful organizations with happy employees," she says.

Jaime Ellertson says you have to "surround yourself with *great* people, not just good people." If you can get people who are better than you at what they do, and lead, not manage them in the process, his experience has been vastly better outcomes. We're talking multibillion-dollar outcomes. But he goes much further—to dominate a market can mean bringing key people with him from company to company.

"I never set out to hire the same people, but if you can use some of the same people that are top performers again and again—whether it's the CEO or a CTO or a head of sales—that helps you accelerate the scale of the business faster. More than anything else, a close management team builds trust, so there isn't a lot of politics," he says.

Glen Tullman has brought his longtime business partner, Lee Shapiro, with him across many businesses, three of which resulted in home run outcomes. "We've had a great partnership. We have complementary skills and built multiple businesses together, including Livongo and Allscripts and 7wireVentures, our early stage digital venture fund," he says. "To do big things that really matter, you need a really solid, committed team, ideally with people who you trust implicitly and will stick with you across various businesses."

WHEN PROCESS TURNS PEOPLE AGAINST EACH OTHER

Steve Raack has spent his career building and growing operations within consumer goods companies from Herbalife to Beautycounter, which experienced 1,500 percent growth in the final two years he spent as Chief Operating Officer.

He says process actually comes before people. "Fix the process, align the expectations, make sure people understand what's really going on," he says. "Because people are there to try to do a good job, but half the time it's the process that causes the problem and then the process turns the people against each other." When people turn on each other, Raack says that's when the culture eats itself and the mentality shifts to "me versus them" or "my agenda versus their agenda."

He says he experienced this firsthand at Sony, which had become a worldwide phenom thanks to brilliant innovations like the Sony Walkman. While he loved the creative setting, Raack remembers "a political type of environment that you have to navigate carefully. I started getting really tired of it. I got to the point where I didn't want my boss's job, or my boss's boss's job. And I didn't want anybody else on the senior leadership team's job. I knew at that point it wasn't for me anymore."

Stints at Herbalife and beauty company Arbonne eventually led Raack to the direct retail skincare and cosmetics brand Beautycounter. He says when he met founder Gregg Renfrew, she "had me at hello." He instantly bought into the company's mission to produce clean products. The company lived its mission to the point of lobbying on Capitol Hill to advocate for safe skincare. He teamed up to lead the charge for creating and putting infrastructure in place to expand into new markets.

In just two years, the business grew from scratch to seventy-five employees. Like other savvy Builders, he knew the failure points that companies typically experience ranging from how cash flow is handled to challenges with technology. He refers to them as "leaky buckets" and proactively makes moves to plug the holes.

BLOCKING AND TACKLING

Before jumping into CEO slots at venture-capital-backed businesses, Charlie Shalvoy served in middle management at industrial giant Emerson Electric, which enjoyed even more quarters of consistent sales growth and profit than General Electric. He remembers top guys flying in on the corporate jet to spend two days with the division executives to review the company's five-year plan. "They were tough. They asked lots of good questions," he says, adding that if you tried to wing it or if you had not done your homework, CEO Chuck Knight would erupt.

Before one of these meetings, Shalvoy was asked to pick up CEO Knight from the airport. He never forgot the advice he got on the drive.

"This is a small division, but, Charlie, the skills you're going to learn in a small division are the same skills you're going to need in a much larger division or a company," Knight told him. "The fundamentals—the blocking and tackling of running a successful business are the same. Just remember two things, Charlie: people and process."

The Builder leverages process as the building blocks to scale. When Shalvoy moved from Emerson to Aehr Test Systems, a $5 million venture capital–funded company out of Menlo Park, California, that made test systems for semiconductor devices, he found that the company had some excellent people, but no processes that would set them up for even greater success.

"The only way they could get products out the door was that these very good people had everything in their heads," he says, remembering trying to get orders shipped for big customers like AMD without any part numbering system or clear way to specify to the manufacturing team what needed to be built. He would walk over to the head of manufacturing to request a product, and she'd ask, "A system like we shipped to Intel a year ago?" He'd say it was about the same and she would say, "Okay, I know what you mean. I'll build you one of those."

One of the first items on Charlie Shalvoy's list was to put together a product configuration ordering guide, then add pricing to all the different options. He tapped into the deep knowledge base in the company while adding process to it. It was moves like this that allowed him to quickly scale the company from $5 million to $50 million while remaining profitable.

Many organizations coast along, at some point becoming stagnant despite movement around them. The Builder brings a fresh view and better practices that often result from exposure to a range of roles and different industry verticals. "What happens in fashion may be applicable to skincare, and what happens in skincare may be applicable to other industries," says Steve Raack, whose experience crosses companies and industries.

RITES OF PASSAGE

It's easy to see a pattern of multiple home runs for successful Builders when viewed with hindsight. And yet. All Builders meet failure at some point. Call it a rite of passage. Anyone and everyone predisposed to solving market problems with products and services will eventually screw up in some way.

By the time he was in his forties Michael Sonnenfeldt had built six different organizations from commercial real estate to nonprofits, but even with multiple wins, losing in even one venture was meaningful. "The failure was nowhere near as big as the success, but from an ego point of view—and for those who know anything about behavioral finance—a dollar lost is a lot more painful than the pleasure of a dollar gained," he says.

For all of Ken Hunt's success in building OneSpan to a multi-hundred-million-dollar leader in the authentication and digital fraud prevention space, he vividly recalls his first acquisition, which turned out to be completely money losing. "I should have been more diligent in my investigation about the business," he says adding that he didn't realize it would be a loss until he closed on the deal. After he was handed the keys and took possession, he discovered it would take about a half million dollars—a big sum relative to what he had bought—to keep the newly acquired company afloat.

Over the years fourteen out of sixteen acquisitions proved to be successful. It dawned on him that he was getting smarter with each acquisition, asking more questions, and getting more referrals. But he had to learn in the school of hit or miss.

Biotechnology leader Bernie Rudnick counts over forty companies he's helped grow or launch, all in healthcare. One recent venture saw him successfully raise $17 million, which eventually yielded $150 million for his investors, but even with that kind of track record, he says his success is "based on a graveyard of errors."

Intrepid Builders use points of failure to evolve. When he purchased the website Time.com out of the blue, Salesforce founder and CEO Marc Benioff said simply that he tried to have a beginner's mind.

"You can't grow if you're not willing to learn," says operations executive Jay Milligan, who helped lead a spinoff from Deloitte, which led to starting a Houston office and growing from zero to $30 million. He then hit the road, opening eight offices from China to Taiwan and growing to $160 million over a five-year span. "Part of learning is accepting the fact that you don't have all the answers and you don't necessarily know everything."

Technology executive Griffin Caprio says, "I found my greatest success by being more human, more transparent, and owning up to the fact that I don't know everything and I'm going to screw up and I'm going to do some things poorly. Instead of trying to shy away from that, let's figure out how to embrace it and use that as an example where people who are on my teams should be able to see that they don't need to be perfect either. They don't need to be infallible, and we're all kind of figuring this out as we go."

Hard lessons come from hands-on experience, and one serial Builder described a public company they ran where not focusing strongly enough on the core product was a big mistake. The market was large, and the team was confident they would be able to get a big slice of it regardless of the product. The key, they thought, was to just out-execute.

Unfortunately, that didn't exactly pan out. "The product was a bit of a mess and it took us almost four years to correct," he remembers. "In today's environment as a public company, it's very difficult to get away with not having stellar returns for multiple years. That probably cost me my job, and it was the best learning experience I could have."

Failure is "probably the strongest experience you can have," he says. "You take away more from it and it molds your career better."

Through those experiences, he learned how to focus his team more on the fundamentals, which he says "aren't to be out-executed or out-smarted. They are fundamentals for a reason."

Successful Builders have an uncanny ability to pivot, continuously taking in market feedback to shift when necessary. Troy Henikoff recalls when he and his partners launched SurePayroll, the original idea wasn't even payroll. They set out to create a human resources services portal for business owners to house documents, regulations, and forms from every state.

When they realized HR needed to connect to payroll, they looked at big players like ADP and Paychex and quickly saw the money to be made in that space. With an online model, they could deliver cheaper than mainframe computers, paper checks, paper reports, and delivery people, so they shifted to payroll, growing the company to process 30,000 small business customers at the point when they sold the company to Paychex.

Stewart Butterfield had a vision for a multiplayer video game but failed to find enough customers. A shift in thinking led to something entirely different: Flickr, which became one of the most popular photo-sharing websites. Yahoo purchased Flickr in 2005, establishing Butterfield's credentials as a rock star leader.

He went at it again, launching another video game company. It also failed to take off, but he and his team were able to take just one component of the game and turn it into Slack Technologies, a leading messaging platform credited with helping teams interact with ease and speed. Five years from its launch, Slack serves nine million weekly active users; has 50,000 paying companies including forty-three of the Fortune 100; and was gobbled up by Salesforce for $27 billion in 2021 in their largest acquisition to date. Butterfield has to be thanking his lucky stars he flopped at video games.

DEVOTED TO FAST GROWTH

Despite inevitable setbacks, Builders are addicted to fast growth and driven to complete the next climb. "You have to love what you're doing," says Jaime Ellertson. "You have to get up in the morning and can't wait to get into the office or can't wait to focus on that next challenge for the business." He launched his first company at the age of twenty, then continued to lead software and SaaS companies, building, selling, or taking public, on repeat.

At some point, growth may slow, or the Builder may feel as if they've scaled Everest and are looking down from the peak with nothing left to conquer. Coincidentally the team may now be so large it exceeds the leader's personal span of control.

That's the moment for many Builders to move on and climb the next mountain—the next market or product or industry. "I love the problem solving, the innovation, the creativity of it. But when it gets to be just operating, I'm ready to move," says Steve Raack, pointing to the moment at Beautycounter when it crossed $100 million in revenue.

At that point, his number two started hiring their number two and he remembers, "It was one of the greatest organizations I was able to be a part of, but I knew at that point it was time to move on." The company then broke his job into three positions, and he left to find his next build.

Lisa Yarnell describes the evolution that happens within the team. "The people inside all know how to do this because they've watched me do it or they've been part of the team to bring it to this place," she says. "They don't remember a time that they didn't do it, or that it wasn't important, or the business didn't grow, or that we wouldn't go into the marketplace, or that we weren't addressing the customer."

Since the institutional memory is now very different from her starting point, she realizes, "They want to run it themselves, and I've worked myself out of a position, because it's become standard operating procedure."

The affirmation going on in the Builder's head is clear: the right market leads to best product or service. Grow it, nurture and mature systems, sell, merge, acquire, IPO, and/or transition to the next leadership team. And then most likely they will seek to repeat.

"I've done a couple of IPOs, but I don't have the patience to be a CEO of a big public company," says healthcare CEO Rudy Mazzocchi. With fifteen successful Builder roles and ninety patents to his credit, he says he would rather build a solution, prove that it works, get it approved, and move to the next challenge.

The Builder Leader		
• Market-oriented	• Agile	• Diligent
• Dominating	• Precise	• Focused
• Hands-on	• Unstoppable	• Detail-oriented
• Persistent	• Scrappy	• Process-driven

In the Trenches with Builders

"If you're not growing, you're dying."
—Russ Reeder

Builders strive to dominate. Level playing field is not in the vocabulary, unless they're facing an entrenched monopoly or government-sponsored player they seek to upend.

Builders bring together the right elements to take a company, industry, or cause to new heights. What's the secret sauce that invigorates extraordinary growth far above the average, the pedestrian, the merely mortal?

This section is a deeper dive into Builders' winning habits and how they quicken the cadence of successful organizations.

Like Fixers, the Builder's style is linear, but that doesn't necessarily make the challenge easier or more obvious. Perhaps the biggest risk for the Builder comes after their first success. Industrial psychologist and leadership coach Bernie Liebowitz explains, "Builders, once they build, they screw up. They think that by building and completing the building that they are masters of the world." He warns that many Builders don't adapt their style like other leadership modes and can come to believe they can build anything.

"Based on the industry, the people, culture, competition, and customers, you have to be able to adapt to different situations," says serial Builder Russ Reeder. "You can't just say, 'I did it this way with the last company. I'm going to do it again with this company.'"

Steve Raack agrees, noting that it's dangerous to not take time to understand the decisions made, what's happening, and the people involved, to then shift to focus on a path forward. "I don't want to talk about the past, I want to honor the past," he says. Rather than pointing fingers, saying, "I can't believe they made this decision," he makes sure to include lots of team feedback. It was a hard lesson for him early on.

Steve recalls his biggest failure: designing a reservation system for Mexicana Airlines. "We built it for them, and we started to roll it out to their reservationists in the field offices, and they rejected it completely," he says. "It was the biggest failure of a project I've ever been on because we didn't take time to build trust and alignment, to help them along. Even though it was the right approach, they just saw us as high-paid people coming in and forcing something down their throat."

MAKE IT MEASURABLE

For many Builders the first step is to shelve the grand ambitions and break down goals into measurable improvement for the team. "We tend to really want to go big, think big, chase the big idea. But if we're being honest, what often ends up is loss of momentum and, frankly, failure down the road because we've bitten off something too large," says Chief Technology Officer Griffin Caprio, who has run many tech teams and finds that smaller deliverables with shorter successive projects increases the likelihood of success.

"If I asked you, hey, where are you going to be in a year, you probably could give me some idea, but it will likely be wrong," Caprio says. "But if I asked, where are you going to be in a month, or a week, or a day, you'd have a better idea. Your degree of success and of being correct will go up."

What he has seen too much of is engineering teams where, he says, "There's always this push for, just give us six months and we'll fix all the problems with the current software—that are completely not our fault—and everything will be better. At the end of three months, what usually happens is people lose momentum, they lose excitement, and now you've got a half-done project that won't ever launch."

Woe is the Builder who forgets their market, falling in love with a perfect product only to be shut out by the audience or customer. Lisa Yarnell has made a habit of putting sales and operations planning meetings in place everywhere she goes. As CEO of Jane Cosmetics, a mass market cosmetics business she acquired from Estée Lauder, she scheduled those meetings once a week and encouraged executives and department heads across marketing, finance, technology, and other areas to attend so they could hear each other and see the dynamics at play.

"You're building collaboration and a horizontal process," she says, adding that it works if leadership attends—not just deputies— so they can "see their relationships, see the collaboration, see the pain points, and help them solve it."

Charlie Shalvoy loves to hold all-hands-on-deck meetings to update the entire company. "We would almost always overcommunicate because the more the team knew about what was going on, the less the rumor mill has anything to grit, to chew on," Shalvoy says adding that he often supplements the staff meeting with monthly brown bag lunch meetings where eight to ten people from different areas of the company had open discussion. If someone was quiet, it was a chance to directly ask questions like, "What's the juiciest rumor you've heard recently?"

Shalvoy says these meetings motivated people to work together much better, feeling they were all on the same page. "We'd be very open. If we had risks or concerns or issues, we'd tell them, so they all knew what we at senior management were working on," he says. "If they knew we were working on it, then they didn't have to worry and could worry about how they get their job done. Build the system they were building or design the next cool new software package or whatever."

YOU NEVER FAIL ON THE LAST DAY

Veteran executive Mike Bartikoski says, "You never really fail in a project on the last day." Being more granular allows you to regroup and pivot from what you've learned, because you haven't committed all your time and all your resources.

With market domination top of mind, Builders zero in on growing sales, getting to highest market share, and generating new products that will attract new customers and markets. Charlie Shalvoy says sales tools are key—the team has to have ammunition in order to be able to effectively present the products and have answers to open questions. He also pays strict attention to pricing.

"If gross margins aren't high enough, we can't support spending large amounts on R&D, which is the lifeblood of any high-technology company. You'd either have to figure out how you can raise your prices or lower your costs," he says.

Shalvoy's next tool in the toolkit is a product road map. "The ideas for new products come from all over the organization, and most importantly from your customer base," he says. "In order to be able to do that job well, I connected a lot with our customers as well as our salespeople and our technical people internally to come up with ideas for the next generation of new products."

With product development in place, Builders focus on process and controls to ensure the organization can meet the demands of quick growth. When Steve Raack jumps into a leadership role, he immediately gloms onto three elements, no matter what product or widget they are selling: order, ship, pay. "If you can't get order, ship, and pay right, your business will implode," he explains. Raack says he's successful because he understands the handoffs.

Handoffs are best illustrated in medical emergencies: "I'm calling 911, because I don't know what's wrong, but the person is dying," Raack says. The 911 operator then hands off to the ambulance. The ambulance shows up and takes the person to the emergency room. The ER takes over, then moves the patient from the ER to the operating room with another handoff, then from OR to the intensive care unit.

"If there are problems in documentation and communication and the handoff, the person's dead," Raack says. "In business, you're not going to die, but if you look at the interactions between process handoffs, well that's where I staked my career."

As a Chief Operating Officer, Raack focuses on the handoffs between ordering, from finance to sales to marketing to shipments to the warehouse. He gives an example of a company where he asked, "Why do you have seven days' inventory of your number one selling item?" It turned out the forecast team didn't give accurate information to the supply team. "You look at the process and can see why it's seven days' supply. So let's go fix the upstream handoffs," he says.

With strong product and process in place, Builders focus on ramping up customer count, which often begins by finding the best point of leverage, the most influential or revered buyer possible. Charlie Shalvoy recalls launching a new semiconductor chip and centering the team's efforts on trying to win over Intel. It wasn't easy. Intel was tough on the engineering team, and if a milestone was missed, Shalvoy says the Intel people beat up on his team. He'd meet with his engineers, who'd ask, "Charlie, why are we doing business with these guys?"

There were other customers presumably more pleasant to work with. But Shalvoy says, "If you want to penetrate a market with a cool new technology, go after the top guys first, because they are the hardest to convince." There may be hurdles for them to adopt your technology, but if they do, everyone else will follow. Intel was the largest microprocessor manufacturer in the world, and when they won the account, six months later they won Samsung, the largest DRAM manufacturer, followed by a stream of other copycat customers. Within three years the product line grew to $200 million.

Builders are scrappy. They fight for their products to survive, thrive, and dominate the marketplace, whether local, regional, national, or global. Cleve Adams was the first executive hired at Websense, a pre-revenue web, data, and email security solution. His revelation came when he read in the *Wall Street Journal* that Compaq laid off seventeen employees for internet abuse.

"I just happened to have an internet anti-abuse product, so I flew to Houston and sat in the lobby of the guy mentioned in the article," Adams remembers. When that guy—the CIO—showed up at his office at 10:00 a.m., Adams told him he was there to solve their problem and was directed to another building where he could talk to the right person. Adams says they weren't about to "buy software from a company that has four guys and a dog running it," but they ultimately cut a deal to buy the software with a guarantee that if Websense went under, Compaq would own the code.

For Adams, it wasn't the dollar volume, it was the reference. Websense went from a pre-revenue firewall reseller to a billion-dollar public company in less than three years, boasting 20,000 corporate customers in eighty-two countries.

Cleve Adams was the first in his family to go to college. He grew up fifty miles east of Los Angeles in what he describes as "cow country." His house was next door to a two-pump gas station that his father ran since he was eighteen years old. Adams had one goal: get out of town.

After college he joined a company and noticed how everything was driven by sales. He decided he was destined to become a sales-driven leader. "You could have the best-running business in the world, and if your sales are flat, you have big problems," he says. "You could have the worst-run business in the world, and if your sales are going through the roof, nobody cares."

Even more important, Adams discovered that having channel partners was the best way to build sales. "I could hire fifty salespeople, but if I could partner with fifty companies with fifty sales people each, I would have that many more selling my product," he says. His focus moved to developing channel programs, thinking about how to offer the perfect combination of a compelling product, market, and partner opportunity.

THE UNSTOPPABLE BUILDER

If a Builder doesn't have an unstoppable nature, they're in the wrong line of work. Rudy Mazzocchi grew his first company, a medical device manufacturer, to 180 people before starting a second company that he sold to St. Jude Medical for $100 million—just twenty-two months after launch. His MO is to team up with surgeons, clinicians, and engineers to bring medical technologies to market. With ninety patents to his credit, he's led fifteen companies and raised nearly $600 million in funding. His pattern is build, expand, sell. And then repeat.

Relentless growth needs a pressure release, in a different way from the Artist's parallel focus. Diana Fongheiser leads one of the fastest growing companies in the US providing therapists to school systems. But with growth can come stress. For Fongheiser the swimming pool is her place of refuge: "I have my angry swim about five days a week and I just get it all out. I leave it all in the pool and I argue, and I pray, and I work it all out and by the time I step out on the pool deck I'm like, okay, now I can have a rational conversation with that attorney."

Christie Hefner, former Chairman and CEO of Playboy Enterprises, reinforces the idea: "Compartmentalizing helps in stressful times, to be able to just put something aside, tackle something else, then come back to the original task or issue."

Gateway Foundation CEO Tom Britton schedules debrief time up front: "I schedule a period every day in the morning, midday, and in the evening to evaluate what I've done, what I need to do, and how I'm doing. Writing stuff down helps me process, analyze, and remember. I almost never go back and read it, but it keeps myself focused."

The vital role of expert Builder is at the core of why free markets work. Every and any organization that has advanced its operations and reached a dominant position, continually striving for more uniqueness, size, financial and market security, and benefit to its stakeholders, can point to one or more successful Builders at the helm.

In Robert's hometown of Chicago, the perennial wannabe Chicago Cubs had a losing streak generations long and had stagnated under the ownership of the Tribune company. Once the Ricketts family took over, it was whole new story, leading to the Cubbies winning the 2016 World Series, breaking a seventy-one-year drought, while the Ricketts rebuilt the stadium and revitalized the entire neighborhood around Wrigley Field.

In Olivia's hometown of Detroit, it took the genius of Quicken Loans founder Dan Gilbert to not only build one of the largest mortgage providers in the US, but then go on to revitalize the Motor City. Gilbert's 17,000 employees live in Detroit, enlivening and enriching the urban experience, while he has purchased much of Detroit's historic downtown business and commercial district.

For organizations that have seen growth stalled, or where no underlying foundation was ever put in place for vital growth, the Builder leader is missing. To achieve exceptional growth or market domination, call in the Builder.

You Know You Are a Builder If ...

✓ You set foundation and structure for an organization, division, product, or service to grow.

✓ You seize new or existing markets.

✓ You are tuned into customer needs and problems to be solved.

✓ You focus intensely on the quality and strength of your product or service.

✓ You weave concepts into improving and adding value.

✓ You are transaction oriented, focusing on the end game of growing, acquiring, IPO or other validation of market value.

✓ You always have a product road map to improve or add new product or services offerings.

✓ You are skilled at building out and strengthening the team.

✓ You view a ceiling as something to be broken through.

✓ You multiply people and processes to create greater efficiency and do more with less.

✓ You have an eye toward expansion whether product, category, customer base, geography, or need fulfillment.

✓ You set and reset best practices.

✓ Your superpower is continual forward movement.

✓ You love the melody of market feedback.

✓ You may lose interest and seek to move to new markets, new products, new needs when market domination is achieved.

4.
THE
STRATEGIST

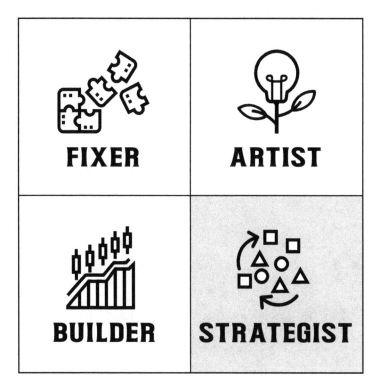

FIXER

ARTIST

BUILDER

STRATEGIST

A Strategist Story: Running at Scale

In 1955, Leonard and Bernice Lavin bought California-based Alberto VO5, a hairstyling product known and loved by Hollywood stars, when it was doing just $400,000 in sales. Over the next thirty years, Alberto-Culver grew to over $500 million in sales through a combination of its consumer products business and Sally Beauty stores. It was considered a Wall Street darling.

But by the early 1990s, the company was at a crossroads. The consumer products portion of the company was falling apart, the board wanted to sell that part of the business, and the company's stock was languishing.

As a publicly held, family-run business, ultimately there came to be three options on the table: One, the Lavins could sell their beloved company. Two, the founding couple could keep running the company, which would mean their daughter, Carol Bernick, who headed the marketing and new products division, and her husband, Howard, who served as COO, would leave the company and seek other leadership opportunities. Or three, the Lavins would move out of operations and let their daughter and son-in-law assume new leadership roles and bring about much-needed changes in the company.

Only one thing was for certain: it was time for a decision.

In 1974, Carol Bernick graduated from college and began canvassing the market for jobs. With an offer from Bristol Myers, she called her dad to say that she wanted to be interviewed for a job at Alberto-Culver. To her dad, she was still his sweet, impressionable young daughter, and he feared that joining the family business would harden her. But Bernick was already all in.

"My mom was a working mom, her mom was a working mom, and their whole life was Alberto-Culver," recalls Bernick. "I mean, there were three kids in my family, but they still worked, and half the time we were sitting there listening to business issues. There were good times, and bad times, and rough times, and wonderful times."

Despite her father's worries about her being exposed to the less-than-glamorous side of operating a business, she knew she wanted to join and carry on the family legacy. She came on board and as she says, "It was crazy hard," but she enjoyed working with her parents.

Bernick started in the marketing department, overseeing company staples. She started to show her chops creating and launching Static Guard, Bakers Joy, Mrs. Dash, and Molly McButter, winning additions to the company lineup that still endure today. The next ten years were spent running the consumer products division representing brands such as VO5, TRESemmé, TCB, Motions, Alberto Balsam, and many more. She came to oversee 3,000 people in the consumer products division.

By the late 1980s, the company hit some serious bumps in the road. The 13 to 14 percent profits on the consumer side had dropped to three percent and continued to plummet. "Our people were not engaged with our products. They didn't understand our brands. We were making no money," remembers Bernick. Retailers were consolidating, making for the most competitive environment they had yet seen.

To compound matters, she says, "Alberto was a place to come and get great experience and then leave." Turnover at Alberto-Culver was twice the industry average, and there were internal disagreements on how the company was approaching their people and potential opportunities.

"We would have nothing without what my parents created. They were very entrepreneurial and very smart, and I have great respect for what they did," says Bernick. "But the world had changed. Selling became focused on the UPC code, and it wasn't just brand and relationship selling, and the consumer package goods giants were wildly outspending us in advertising."

Bernick found herself at odds with the way things were being run and was convinced they were spread too thin and focused on too many brands. While her father pointed to the fact that they were in 120 countries, she knew they were only big in seven or eight. She felt they should be spending more money on Alberto-Culver's biggest brands in their largest markets.

"My dad is a salesman, and he didn't really think about profits much," she says. "He was always going after the next sale and figured profits would take care of themselves. Businesses go out of business that way, right?"

The only thing keeping the company afloat was a division that had been acquired in 1969, the Sally Beauty company. It was a machine, rolling up the fragmented beauty industry. "We'd acquired twenty-two stores here, thirty-six here, forty-five there and trekked around the country doing this," says Bernick. "Acquiring two or three chains every year for decades was automatic growth and fed the engine easily."

In 1994, revenues hit an all-time high at $1.22 billion, with the majority of the $44.1 million in profits driven by Sally Beauty rather than by consumer products.

Carol and Howard Bernick put to her parents the need to make changes in the company. The board supported that. A two-year board-negotiated change reviewed three options: to sell, keep things as they were, or go through a management change. Carol's father, Leonard, was in his seventies, and a decision finally was made.

Leonard stepped out of operations to concentrate on his board chairman role, and Bernick's husband at the time, Howard, was named as CEO. The company was completely restructured into three units: Alberto-Culver USA, Alberto-Culver International, and Sally Beauty. Carol Bernick took the title of President of Alberto-Culver USA, and later International as well, with a laser focus on turning things around.

"We had to make some money in the consumer products business, or we were going to be out of business," says Bernick. Within the first month of taking on the new role, she worked with the engineers, package development people, and production line workers to figure out how to rework VO5 shampoo.

"It was our biggest brand—it was selling for ninety-nine cents—and was running our factories around the clock, but we were making absolutely no money on it," she says. Thanks to the new packaging and better operations, "within one year we took profits on VO5 from 1 cent a bottle to 4.5 cents a bottle. We were back in business."

In addition, she put more financial controls in place. "We started doing profitability by account, profitability by brand, and bonusing our executives and sales force on same," she says. "It was complex, but there were some pretty fundamental things that were easy fixes when we took over their business."

It wasn't about cost cutting or new products. "I say to everybody the single biggest new product I ever introduced was the culture change at Alberto, which people became hugely engaged in," she says. "It was my mission, my purpose, my everything."

In 1993, right before taking the new role heading up the US business, Bernick created an initiative called Workplace 2000, setting a goal to become a top company to work for in America by the year 2000. It was a big goal, especially coming from a place where a survey of employees revealed wide-reaching dissatisfaction.

"People would describe me as somebody with strong creative and strategic skills, who truly cared about her people," Bernick says. This passion for her people, brands, and for providing creative solutions to difficult problems was something that evolved throughout her career, and she points to a YPO forum (Young Presidents' Organization) of executives who met regularly to discuss business, life, and leadership as a major source of influence.

"There were two women in this group and the rest were men, but the most impressive thing to me, that I came to realize knowing the group so intimately, is that women and men are basically the same," she says. "While men don't show it the same way, they have the same emotions and feelings, the same tears, the same love of their kids, the same love of their family as all the women I knew."

It was this insight that led Bernick to remake the culture of Alberto into a family-first culture. "My lawyers didn't like me to say it, but I didn't care which twelve hours of the day you gave us," she says. "If your kid had a softball game at three o'clock in the afternoon, go. My daughter played competitive softball, and I was going to go—and you were going to watch me go—because nothing is more important in this world than your kids, and at the end of the day, when everything else is finished, no one ever says they wished they'd spent more time at work."

That said, Bernick points out that they "were still an extremely competitive, hardworking organization where people probably worked harder than they did anywhere else in their life."

Carol Bernick's YPO executive forum has now stayed together for twenty-five years, and she emphasizes the significance they played early in her leadership journey. "I swear to you, it just kind of hit me after getting to know these people and watching them grow their companies," she says. "I changed my leadership style to be willing to show empathy, emotional intelligence, and caring compassion. I realized that you could lead a company that way and be just as effective as a hard-nosed crazy leader."

When she unlocked the key to her management style, Bernick also rolled out what she called a "walk in my shoes culture."

"We talk at great length that everybody has a higher power, whether it's your parents, or your church, or your kids, or whatever," she says. "But I always believed the students involved in extracurricular activities brought more to the table, so to speak, than students who were uninvolved in their schools or communities. People who had a more well-rounded life and believed in a purpose made better employees." A walk in my shoes culture meant giving people the freedom to be who they were, to be proud of what they were feeling, and to share it.

This cultural makeover truly stuck with the creation of a new role called the Growth Development Leader (GDL). Seventy people across the company were given this role to act as mentors and encourage not only company growth, but growth at an individual level. Bernick and the executive team met with all the GDLs every six weeks to gain insight into questions and concerns within the company, to prioritize major initiatives, and to ensure there was transparency about sales and earnings, new programs, products, and more.

"I am totally a hundred percent convinced it's the people that make it happen," Bernick says. It translates into her leadership style where she walked the floor, talking to everybody and asking questions like, What do you need? How can we help? What do you do really well? What would you like to do better? How are your people? I don't come in with all the answers," she says. "I come in and try to figure out who the players are, who I want to team with . . . I put ridiculously smart people around me who are smarter than I am and make sure they are competent and happy in their job. I'm the person who pulls the team together to look at all the issues and try to find the quickest way to a solution."

Though the culture was rapidly transforming for the better, the following years were not devoid of issues. "We had an aerosol plant blow up. It was not ours, but a vendor's plant in Mexico that had not followed protocol. Three people died. It was horrible," she remembers.

In the midst of crisis and tragedy, the new shift in culture and mindset that infiltrated the company did, however, drastically change how people responded to challenges. "We jumped in front of it and went to the Mexican government to pay for those people's funerals and helped support their families. We put a community center together where we installed a playground and park," says Bernick. "Lots of people used this supplier, but, still, you're responsible." Despite the fact that it was not just Alberto-Culver product in those plants, they took the approach of trying to be as compassionate as possible.

The lessons learned did not stop there. The number one ingredient in Alberto-Culver's biggest product, TRESemmé hairspray, was discontinued, followed by a number of other government changes in ingredient regulations. Formulas needed to be reworked, and the company had to pivot. Alberto-Culver chose the highest quality alternative to reconfigure the product even though it hit profits hard; whereas, their competitors did not. By making this fundamental change, they grew to be number one in the market.

Bernick recalls—not fondly—of a time when the team at the manufacturing plant for Mrs. Dash found a moth in a gallon drum of peppers sent over from a supplier. Everyone from legal to the FDA was brought in to inspect what was going on, but she said even if the pepper supplier was responsible, it was Alberto-Culver's brand and they had to own up. "You have to recall it, right?" she says. "It wasn't a mandatory recall. It was a voluntary recall, but we pulled it back."

While moths in Mrs. Dash wouldn't have harmed anyone, the surprise of them flying out of the bottle may have caused a heart attack.

"Mistakes happen and things get screwed up," but Carol Bernick's philosophy is that people should be candid about business problems and should feel like they can share problems so that they can collectively figure out a solution. "I am an open kimono," she says. "There are no secrets. We're not going to hide it. We're just going to fix it and figure it out . . . we're all paid big bucks to figure it out."

Even in interviewing top VPs for the management team, Bernick would always ask one question: What's one of the worst things to ever happen to you in business? Those who could own up to massive blunders showed they could be trusted.

The years to come were marked by more big changes. Sally Beauty hit around 2,000 stores and Alberto-Culver products were doing well, but having disparate products and services within one public company added complexity. "L'Oréal and Procter were my biggest competitors to the consumer division, yet they were our biggest customers at Sally," she remembers. "We would have major chains refuse to do business with us because the Sally store had opened in the same market, in the same mall. I can't tell you the number of meetings that started with a fifteen-minute conversation about Sally instead of our products because a new Sally store had just opened up in their market."

It just was not working as currently structured, so in 2006, they initiated a Reverse Morris Trust, breaking off Alberto-Culver and Sally Beauty into two separate public companies.

It was a big accomplishment and the right thing to do for both businesses. "In a public company, you're always worrying about the next quarter, the next quarter, and the next quarter," says Bernick. "Even when you have fantastic results it's hard to celebrate. But my best days were the days that we took time to celebrate with our people, and we turned it from people uninvolved to people who loved working there and really felt they made a difference."

L'Oréal, Procter, Unilever, and Kao were the four majors in the 1980s with around thirty-five companies in a second tier. By the time 2010 came around, three were left standing and everyone else had been absorbed.

When Bernick heard through the grapevine that Unilever was thinking about making a play for them, she immediately got to work finding out if the rumors were true. TRESemmé had been doing so well they had taken it to England where they had achieved significant market share. They were preparing to take it to Brazil and Japan next and, along with international expansion of other products, were gearing up to invest tens of millions of dollars, a number that would take their earnings down for the first time in ten years. Bernick knew that if a possible sale was on the table, it had to be when earnings were strong.

"We looked at ourselves and said this is probably what we need to do," she says, adding that Unilever did not have a big shampoo business at the time in the United States. They concluded it was also the *only* company left that could have even acquired Alberto, given the Justice Department would consider everyone else too large.

The $3.7 billion cash acquisition of Alberto-Culver by Unilever was announced in September 2010 and closed in May 2011. The exit was bittersweet, having to say farewell to a family legacy.

Bernick has continued to have impact as a leader. A year after the sale, she was asked to step into the Chairwoman of the Board role at Northwestern Healthcare. In partnership with CEO Dean Harrison, Northwestern tripled the size of its healthcare system, transitioning from a fine regional hospital into one of the best healthcare systems in the US.

Carol Bernick, having already created the Friends of Prentice in 1985, a nonprofit dedicated to improving the quality of women's healthcare through support of Chicago's major women's hospital, translated her love of people and service to others into her founding of two additional charities: Enchanted Backpack, which provides school supplies, thousands of books, winter coats, athletic equipment, and art materials to a minimum of 20,000 students every year in under-resourced schools across Chicago and NW Indiana; and CC's Wishlist, a unique program utilizing Bernick's corporate buying experience to purchase brand-new, quality clothing, socks and underwear, shoes and boots, winter outerwear, bedding, small household goods, and toys and sports equipment that are donated to worthy nonprofits in Illinois and Florida.

The Strategist Leadership Mode

Cadence is mantra for the Strategist.

There is a cadence—a heartbeat—in every organization. Strategist leaders can feel the rhythm and beat, working to sustain, vitalize, and quicken the pace. It's the lifeblood of the organization.

"I am creating a heartbeat in whatever I'm working on for the organization," says Mike Zawalski, a Quaker Oats veteran executive who now leads private equity–backed businesses. "A business needs to have a cadence. It needs to have a rhythm. There is a cadence around strategy. There is a cadence around operational excellence, culture, and how people are treated."

The successful Strategist navigates the complexity of large organizations, if not with ease, then with increasing mastery. "When you know you have to increase the organization's cadence, you think about everything tangential as well," says Zawalski. "It may be new capabilities or a different product set. It may be a different management team or channel strategy, but when you start to think about heartbeat as an analogy, if it's like the human heart, then if you want to run farther, you've got to train, you've got to create different muscle strengths. I view it that way because it allows me at a very high level to think structurally about what I need to do to affect the business and what capabilities I need to work on that directly improve the heartbeat, if you will, which is that cadence or rhythm that creates value."

"You have to be strategic. You have to be a visionary," says Susan Sentell. "You're setting the direction for the organization that you're leading." As President of an $8 billion business unit at Sprint, Sentell was able to grow market share and achieve more than 10 percent annual revenue and profit growth. But leading 3,000 employees was not a trivial task. She had a keen ability to engage with employees, build high-performing teams, create consensus, and motivate the team to make it happen. "It's important to have that good balance of strategy, but also the ability to marshal your resources, coordinate the organization toward achieving those goals," she says.

In building operations, teams, divisions, functions, and perhaps a global footprint, many Strategists also identify with the Builder label, but we make a distinction: Builders form, forge, and produce a structure that can stand on its own. Strategists enhance the multiplicity of structures—building roads, towns, networks, connectivity, and empires—that can become vast or complex at scale.

"You get to this point where you can't have your hands on everything. You've got to step back and be more of a conductor and less of a doer, but you've got to make sure it gets done," says Janine Davidson, who began her career as a pilot in the US Air Force. Then followed fourteen years in Washington and completion of a doctorate. In 2016, she was appointed by the President of the United States as the thirty-second Under Secretary of the United States Navy and Chief Management Officer for the Navy and Marine Corps.

Dr. Davidson says too many leaders want to "play with the toys" and end up diving too deep into the weeds. With a $190 billion budget and 900,000 people to oversee, she views leading a complex organization as a challenging puzzle, or a system of systems. Finding the nodes in the system that have the most cascading effect on change is key, and for her that means trusting and building up other leaders within the organization.

SEEING THE ENTIRE FIELD

Call them captain, director, quarterback, or conductor, the Strategist leader sees the entire field, team, and stakeholders and activates a battle plan that gets everyone moving according to a clear mission, common goals, and direction. In a large organization, an incremental change—even a small shift in play—can have a significant effect. President Barack Obama once observed that if the massive ship of state was course-corrected by just two degrees, it might look in short order to be unaffected but, if seen over time, would in fact have completely changed direction.

Having responsibility for thousands of employees along with 15,000 agents and $14 billion in revenues at Farmers Insurance, former President Mhayse Samalya focused on the cumulative effect. "To move the organization, the best way to do that is to figure out where the motivation points are for people," he says. "They're not all the same and they're not all the things that I personally believe in that motivate me. If you've got 10,000 people and their performance moves in the smallest little amount, that smallest amount times 10,000 is enormous."

The Strategist is a master at getting buy-in to a bigger mission and vision and keeping the organization accountable for forward movement and results. Though skilled at choosing, coordinating, and marshaling resources, Susan Sentell says it goes beyond that. A good leader must capture the hearts of the people: "Integrity and trustworthiness is important and that goes back to people trusting you, people wanting to follow, people wanting to believe in your vision and engage in it." She adds that compassion is a key trait.

People development, both personal and collegial, is an important and widely shared sentiment among Strategists, who often gain drive and purpose from the people they surround themselves with. Jack Welch famously said that "people development should be a daily event, integrated into every aspect of your regular goings-on," sharing in his autobiography that he got a lot more satisfaction from working within GE than from working outside with, say, customers.

Samalya shared a similar sentiment. "I can't say I always got a kick out of producing the best result hitting our plan," he says. "The thing that gave me the biggest kick was really always about people and people development."

ORGANIZATION AND TEAM COME FIRST

His best day as a leader, says Samalya, is when someone he mentored gets a big promotion—regardless of whether that person still works for his company. He prides himself on having mentored people who have gone on to become Presidents and CEOs of other companies. "I've always tried to tell people, look, my job, my fiduciary responsibility is to this company, but I also care about you as a person. We've got a litany of jobs here and my job is to try to figure out what is the best match for you that's going to help the company and help you," he says.

That philosophy may or may not fit within the confines of the jobs available at the company, but Samalya finds that demonstrating to people that you care about them as a person is powerful even if they're not a fit for the organization. "I actually had someone I had to terminate from the company, who I ran into years later and they said, 'What you did was the best thing for me,'" he says.

Barry Zekelman is CEO of steel manufacturer, Zekelman Industries—a company he took over when he was just nineteen years old after his dad passed away, leaving him with a failing business and five employees. Zekelman transformed the company into a $4.5 billion revenue leader in North American steel construction products and is now well known as a champion for manufacturing in the US.

You can sense it's a little hard for him to fully put into words the passion he feels for what he does, the people he surrounds himself with, and the impact his company has in communities where his plants employ hundreds of workers in each plant. Whether expanding plants into small towns or more populated areas, he has seen kids graduate from high school, come to work for the company, and flourish. One of those high schoolers started out running a cutoff saw and is now President of a $2.8 billion division of Zekelman.

"I'll tell you what makes me the most proud," he says referring to his 2,700 employees. "When I watch them make decisions that I would have made. And then decisions that they are making better than I ever could have made. And I just love that. I just know we're going to keep succeeding."

It's seeing what his team is capable of that energizes him, and his goal is to ensure that everyone has decision-making power to the point that the little bead of sweat runs down their head. "I want them to feel that," Zekelman says. "And that's like training. You're working your mind. You're working your capabilities. You excel at that or you don't, but I'm going to give you that chance. But I would also say big dreams. It all comes back to big dreams."

Dan Epstein is driven by being able to be creative, to mentor people, to build relationships with clients, focus on the future, and bring together people to think about that future in new ways. In leading a service provider to insurance organizations, Epstein says, "I get to provide a meaningful career to a lot of people who are all supporting families and build a culture that treats people with respect, dignity, and is seeking to provide them with upward mobility." He sees his career as a calling because it satisfies so many of the traits that give meaning in life.

The best Strategists have a genuine desire to serve, putting the needs of the organization and team first. An accomplished Fortune 100 CEO describes that desire: "If I close the day up and I don't feel like I've added any value either to the projects I'm working on or for my family or the people around me—if the day was consumed with tasks that aren't creating value or energy—it is not a great day."

Mhayse Samalya says, "I think we all have some innate sense of what's right, what's wrong, what should be done, what shouldn't be done. My worst day is when people are really dealing in self-interest." He has an intrinsic sense of working on behalf of the greater good, the greater whole of the organization. He describes the opposite this way: "They're not dealing in the best interest. They're not trying to get to the right answer. They're trying to get to what makes them look good."

Fortune 1000 executive Susan Sentell shares in the dynamic to serve: "We are leaders but we're also just a member of the organization. Everybody has their role. I think I always viewed that I'm part of the team, and the team achieves."

Verinder Syal, who served in senior management at Quaker Oats, says, "I never put my own career beyond what I thought the business needed, which were two things: what the customer needed, and what commitments that we as a group made to our company." He admits that early on, "All I wanted in my life someday was to have a job as a manager with two people reporting to me. That was my dream." He succeeded, and then some. His path took him to directing 5,000 people with responsibility for hundreds of millions of dollars in sales.

DEVELOPING LEADERSHIP CHOPS

Strategists point to their mentors and the value of learning and development programs as empowering waypoints for increasing opportunities, responsibilities, and success in leadership roles. The corporation is described as nurturing and career shaping. At the center of their experience and success it is the source of their gratitude.

"My path was one of really working to assemble the skill set and then working in particular functions and in particular areas of the business that were focused on growth," says one Fortune 250 executive. "I was fortunate to work for a company that culturally looked to move people around and provide a diversity of experiences. I was just thrilled and thankful to have the opportunity to work with such a talented group of people across so many different functions."

The Strategist leader's loyalty to an organization shines through as the opportunity to intentionally work to develop skills across different functional areas presents itself—from finance to operations to marketing and sales.

When Barry Zekelman was thirty-nine, he cut a deal to partner with a private equity fund, The Carlyle Group. When a good friend asked Zekelman why he would give up some of the company, he said, "Because at the end of this, I'm going to come out with more knowledge and be more lethal than I ever was before."

In 2011 he bought back Carlyle's stake and looks back on what he learned. "I grew up with nothing. I had to do it by the seat of my pants," he says. "So Carlyle taught me board decorum. They taught me how to maneuver through Wall Street. They taught me how to recruit people. They taught us corporate governance. All of those things that I didn't really know."

While at both AT&T and Sprint, Susan Sentell found that whenever there was a department that needed help, she was deployed, never staying for more than two years before going to a different area of the business to start something up or solve another complex problem. "That feeds me and it was probably good that people that I worked for figured that out. I love complex problem solving," she says. "I enjoy being able to think at a high level, but across multiple areas of the business."

But let's not sugarcoat that everything's kumbaya, lovey-dovey in major corporations. Verinder Syal recalls a corporate culture revolving around dressing well and making good presentations. Performance? It was optional. "That was a shock, and became my competitive advantage without my knowing it," he says. "I was one guy who always delivered what he said, honestly and ethically. But I didn't dress well like they did, and I sure as hell didn't listen to people like they did, and I didn't go along with people like they did. But I delivered."

Like Syal, many Strategists don't necessarily begin with ambitions to climb every mountain. We heard Microsoft CEO Satya Nadella say during a speech that he recalled being questioned by board members during the CEO selection process, asking why he wanted the top job, and he replied, "Are you sure you *want* me as CEO?" Whether stepping into a CEO or other leadership role, a sense of reluctance or satisfaction with their current role can still exist before leaping at the opportunity.

Master tactician Ron Adams, top assistant coach of the NBA's Golden State Warriors, was quoted as saying, "I try to be an artisan.

There is a purity . . . a virtue in being a craftsman and having a craft. It's the nuts-and-bolts stuff that appeals to me, and the relationships. Plus, quite frankly, I don't think, until the last five or six years of my life, I exhibited the flexibility to be a head coach. The level where I've found myself is just perfect."

Author Sam Walker described Dwight Eisenhower as someone who "had zero interest in running for President but was entered in the 1952 New Hampshire primary by supporters without his permission. As the 'I Like Ike' movement snowballed, he relented." Walker cites other examples of reluctant superscalers who led without big personalities, including Paul Polman, Unilever's widely admired CEO, who said he "never wanted to be a CEO."

Janine Davidson says she never fully intended to make a full twenty- or thirty-year career out of the military. "I didn't love the Air Force, but I wasn't sure what I wanted to do," she says. "I love that I did it. It was a great experience. I had a love-hate thing. It was very rigid for me on the one hand, and on the other hand it was also very exciting. I loved flying. I loved traveling. I loved the people that I worked with. I look back on that experience and I realize how much I learned."

Dr. Davidson adds that everyone has an area of expertise, which is different from a skill set. Her area of expertise was national security, foreign affairs, and military options. She discovered that her skill set was leadership. When she caught the leadership bug, she became confident that she could take her skill set into different industries and arenas.

After serving as Under Secretary of the Navy, Janine Davidson accepted the position of President of Metropolitan State University of Denver, which was a shock to her team at the Pentagon. Moving from a role overseeing hundreds of thousands of people to 1,100 university faculty and staff seemed like an unconventional move, but she was drawn to the opportunity.

"I wanted to lead an organization that was mission driven, and President of a university very much fits that," she says. "The processes and procedures and the game that we play at the university is very similar to the Pentagon. The budget process is very similar, and you have all kinds of stakeholders coming to the table."

Her willingness to seek new learning and explore different paths points to the Strategist wiring and adaptability. Psychologist and leadership expert John Behr says, "There are perhaps fifteen or so competences that are essential for every leader, but a few that are more essential for a leader of an organization that's globalizing: flexibility, tolerance of ambiguity, and adaptability. These relate to creativity, which is a willingness to be open to possibilities."

THE EVOLUTION OF THE STRATEGIST

Verinder Syal has taught entrepreneurship at Northwestern University and mentors students, sharing lessons learned while leading Quaker. "Most people don't have confidence in themselves," he says. "There's a sense of disbelief. We are told all the things we cannot do. We just don't have enough people in our lives who give us the sense of 'I believe in you. You can do more.' So we have to unlearn all the stuff we've been told we can't do. That to me is the essence of leadership."

Psychologist and leadership coach Bernie Liebowitz highlights the evolution of many leaders of large organizations: "Strategists are able to change, and how they change and what they change to is not something that is dramatic. It's just that there is a self-consciousness about themselves that appreciates the fact that as you grow from leadership over 1,000 to 10,000 to 50,000 employees, you *have* to change." Strategists can grow and serve at one company for a long time, usually aided by being cross-functionally trained.

In 1985 Shawn Score started as a salesperson at Best Buy, at that time a twelve-store chain before the big box era. Moving up through the ranks, he went from assistant manager to store manager to district manager to regional manager, while jumping from one part of the US to another.

"I think I fell in love with the company after meeting with the founder a few times and getting mentored along the way," says Score. "It really boils down to the people and the mission of continually changing our operating model and our value propositions that were necessary to compete in today's environment."

Over the next fifteen years, Score reported directly to the CEO as Senior Vice President where he led initiatives ranging from running the sales development department to leading Best Buy's mobile joint venture. He recalls, "I actually never interviewed for a job. I was always just given the job and was being groomed at one point to be the CEO." He realizes that as he took the company through ten major operating model changes and annual cost-cutting efforts involving thousands of people, his own style of leadership was also changing, and it was the execution versus the planning phase that gave him his energy.

Dan Epstein recalls that in the early years at ReSource Pro he served at some point in every job slot at the company. Within a year, he stepped into the CEO role and turned the company into one of the fastest growing insurance industry service providers, reaching number 57 on the Inc. 5000 list for growth just a few years later. At that point, the challenges of getting credibility in the market, establishing messaging, or getting marketing infrastructure in place quickly shifted, which meant Epstein and his team had to evolve.

"The bottlenecks are changing all the time," he says, describing that in the midst of such rapid growth, the bottleneck became how to deliver service to all of their clients. He realized, for example, that every client having its own team leader was not scalable, so he made a change to share team leaders across clients and shift their focus to spending more time creating deep connections with clients. And then the bottleneck would change again. Twenty employees grew to 5,000 in locations ranging from China to India to Lincoln, Nebraska.

"The opportunity as well as the challenge as a leader is to manage the entire portfolio, which requires some mode switching," describes one Strategist who led the US division of a healthcare company, with 3,000 employees reporting to him. "The ability to go from one mode to another is important. As a Strategist you're both leading the overall direction but then gearing some efforts up, adding fuel to others, and managing different parts of the business."

The Strategist is a leader who grows over the course of their career into successively larger formal roles and responsibilities in revenue, organizational complexity, and people management. Joe Mansueto, founder and chairman of financial services powerhouse Morningstar, has described how he was able to grow in his own capability from conceiving a business plan in his apartment to leading 4,000 employees worldwide thirty years later.

By engaging in a continual act of learning where he read and analyzed how success was achieved by more accomplished, "bigger" leaders, he consciously expanded and changed his own style of leadership, reinventing himself again and again.

Jeff Chalovich spent thirty-three years in the corrugated packaging industry, rising through the ranks from salesman at Nekoosa to President of WestRock's packaging division, where he helped take the company from $800 million to $12.5 billion, part of a $19 billion industry leader. He reflects, "My leadership style changed over time. I built great teams but I became a much better empower-er as time went on and really became more of a thought partner, business partner, coach, counselor, developer of people."

As Barry Zekelman's role evolved at his company, he reflects: "When I see people advance and grow—test themselves and grow into different positions and make decisions—it's funny because I have to recuse myself a lot of times." He says, "I can't keep sticking my finger in. It's very hard when you were the quarterback, and then you're the coach, and then you're the general manager, now you're up in the press box, you still want to go down on the field and throw a ball."

SELF-OBSOLESCING FROM ROLE TO ROLE

The nimble corporation of the future may well require Strategists, as they rise through the ranks, to essentially self-obsolesce themselves, to continually increase the efficacy and completeness of both their own internal functions as well as their product and service offerings. A kind of metamorphosis needs to take place for a rising Strategist, a sluffing off the old, the former leader and role, in favor of a more evolved and capable new.

Rob McClung heads up operations centers at Stripe, after having run Google's support for Google Commerce and other functions over a seven-year span. While at Google he realized, "Even though the title will stay the same, I will not be doing the same thing in twelve months. I'll be running people, but the people will be doing totally different things."

Successful Strategists become leadership virtuosos, showing strength as listeners, problem solvers, communicators, collaborators, and motivators. Their experience and arc in their careers could take them through a number of leadership modes.

FedEx founder Fred Smith is arguably the quintessential demonstration of a complete metamorphosis, evolving from idea generator to Builder to Fixer to superscaling Strategist. Stories of FedEx's early struggles are legend. Millions of dollars in debt, and with just $5,000 in the bank, they hit a point where they could not afford to fuel the planes. No planes, no deliveries.

In an act of desperation, Smith flew to Las Vegas to give the blackjack table a go to keep the company afloat. While a seemingly insane move to put the entire company at risk, $5,000 turned into $27,000, and he bought himself more time. Forty-five years later, Smith is still CEO, directing 227,000 employees, generating $65 billion in revenues.

To continue to grow a company that many might see as already arrived, long-term vision is a strong driver for the Strategist leader. Fixers and Artists start short and hope to inspire long-term vision. Builders may think they are long players, but usually aim at a market need in the foreseeable future and within their grasp. Strategists, meanwhile, know that even the giants are ripe for disruption, so they are continually thinking about how to rank high in market share and remain relevant years from now.

IT'S ALL ABOUT VISION AND MISSION

After running the Spanish mobile phone company, Airtel Movil, José Ignacio Sánchez Galán was recruited to Iberdrola, the second largest Spanish utility. The company had assets in hydro power and nuclear, with some oil- and coal-fired power-generation plants in Spain and a bit in Latin America. In widely reported news, Galán made the bold move to close all of their oil and coal plants and instead become one of the largest wind energy companies in the world.

As he told *Harvard Business Review*, "Competitors thought I was crazy. Wind power was in its infancy, and solar was prohibitively expensive, so no one understood why I wanted to target renewable energy. Regulators raised a skeptical brow. Some senior executives retired or left." This ability to see down the field paid off. Over the two decades Galán's been at the helm, Iberdrola expanded into dozens of countries on four continents, serving 100 million people.

Strategists feel the pulse of the world and their industry, knowing that sitting still amounts to stagnation. "In my business, I'm thinking several years ahead because we are in an industry that's changing fairly rapidly," Dan Epstein says. "If I think about where the insurance industry is headed, where our clients are headed, and how those organizations are going to be managed and run in the future, there are changes that are coming, and probably in the next ten years it's going to look quite different."

When Epstein joined ReSource Pro there were just twenty employees, and he was quickly entrusted with the CEO role, ramping up growth to its current strength of 5,000 worldwide. This is a common evolution and transformation of a Strategist, from team Builder to confirmed Strategist.

There's no blah blah in Epstein's mission: he knows where he needs to take his team and where he should make investments today that will transform their business and position them to be at the forefront of whatever the industry looks like tomorrow. Epstein says, "While some investments need to see an ROI within five years, others need to start now in order to have an impact in eight to twelve years. You have to be able to bring a broad number of your team and board with you in seeing that vision."

THE PRESSURE FOR CONSISTENT RESULTS

Strategists answer to shareholders, internal constituencies, and board members, notching up the pressure to achieve consistent growth.

"Let's say you're at three or four hundred million in revenue: it's a very different set of skills to move that along to $410, $420, $430 million and to be disciplined enough to find those small incremental opportunities and to enforce the discipline in sales and marketing to continue to drive consistent growth, to drive value for the stakeholders involved," says Chief Operating Officer Mike Bartikoski.

Strategists' decisions to drive those incremental gains in revenue or earnings can be gut wrenching. When Shawn Score was elevated into the role of President of Best Buy's US stores, a global executive team was already in place whose sole focus was on driving the stock price. By that point Score had been with Best Buy so long, he had seen the company grow from 800 employees to 135,000 and $50 billion in sales. He was invested in the mission and people so deeply that when cuts had to be made, it wasn't easy on him.

"It was absolutely awful when I knew the names of the people that we were going to lose," he remembers. "Either people that I moved to markets who stayed there and took over for me, or people I had groomed, developed, and raised. When you are writing the plan and you can see the face of the people it's going to impact, it's heart wrenching."

In high-profile organizations, the world seems to be watching the leader's every move, every word, every tweet. When a passenger was dragged off a United Airlines flight, five million people watched the video, and the company's value dropped by about $1 billion in the following days.

Strategists have a tough time surviving mistakes, whether or not they were to blame. Paul Polman, CEO of $62 billion Unilever, was summarily ousted after losing a fight over Unilever's London headquarters location in the wake of the United Kingdom's decision to exit the European Union.

John Flannery was given just eleven months to turn around GE, then was sacked. Bob Diamond resigned as CEO of Barclays after the pressure of the 2012 Libor scandal, despite reports that he had no knowledge of interest rate submissions being manipulated and that regulators were alerted in advance but failed to act.

President Barack Obama noted that during his presidency, there were always five or more crises demanding attention simultaneously. Nonstop—day in, day out—morning, noon, and night. Running a big organization means more people; more divisions, departments, and teams; more markets; more complexity; and more possibilities for crises.

Rob McClung, thinking of his role at Stripe and Google before that, describes his worst day as coming into a situation where you could have anticipated something you didn't. "When you can't predict that failure point as an engineer, that's really frustrating," he says. "With all the data and information we have, it's just not acceptable."

McClung routinely focuses on identifying potential failure points, knowing that for corporations big and small, where command of data provides a competitive advantage (and doesn't that mean pretty much every organization?), mistakes, omissions, and simply being asleep at the switch can be potentially cataclysmic. Look at examples like the Equifax data hack, Target's 2013 credit card breach (Target's CEO was let go shortly thereafter), the 2020 SolarWinds hack that hit hundreds of US government agencies and departments, or the Columbia pipeline ransomware hack of 2021. Cybersecurity is now a constant, recurring challenge that spares no company, industry, or government.

When crisis does hit, the successful Strategist leader goes into action, putting everything on the line. Sam Walker, author of *The Captain Class: A New Theory of Leadership* writes about George Washington at the Battle of Princeton in 1777. Opening fire from

British soldiers sent the Continental Army into a panic. Washington drove into withering fire, the largest target in sight, staying in front of his men. Yet he didn't flinch. Walker writes of officers at the scene who caught the General's infection of bravery and pressed on. Washington was a combination of relentless effort and emotional control.

We all talk about leading by example, and being vulnerable, but what does that really mean in the modern age? Just how much risk does the average leader take in the course of their career?

STRATEGISTS KEEP A COOL HEAD

When Mhayse Samalya got into the business world, he realized his upbringing gave him skills in areas that others didn't necessarily have. He was the firstborn child in a family where both of his parents had to work. "Early on in my life I ended up not necessarily wanting any kind of leadership role, but really it being thrust on me," he remembers. "I had five brothers and sisters, and generally when problems came up, they fell on me to fix or be on top of things. And so, I would say I developed at an early age calmness in the face of fire."

When one of his siblings got hurt or didn't show up at home, Samalya says he kept a cool head to figure out what to do, whom to call, or even how to get an ambulance when one of his brothers or sisters got a little too adventurous. It's this calmness, ability to look at events more objectively, and strength in taking in different data points to synthesize them into something meaningful that transferred to the business world.

Tom Britton leads 1,500 healthcare staff at Gateway Foundation, the largest nonprofit addiction treatment service provider in the US. "I believe in the mission of saving lives," he says. "Even if I have a totally shitty financial quarter, we would have served 18,000 people in those ninety days. That's pretty awesome."

Organizations like Gateway, fueled by a strong sense of mission, can become unstoppable. During the toughest period of the 2020 pandemic onslaught, Gateway never slowed down—adding 30,000 people served.

Rick Smith, founder and CEO of Axon and creator of the nonlethal Taser weapon, has a two-word mission: eliminate bullets. Love or hate Taser, but his mission is clear.

For many companies, mission can sound like a grab bag of values that don't necessarily relate to the true intent and purpose of the company. Serving in leadership roles at PepsiCo, Coca-Cola, and Hershey, Mike Bartikoski notes that whether a company is talking about valuing people or being committed to sustainability, people are watching to see if companies truly practice what they preach.

FIND THE HEARTBEAT, SET THE CULTURE

Mission is goal one for Strategists, but in broad strokes corporate mission statements can all start sounding the same. Notice how every commercial aired during the COVID pandemic of 2020 repeated the same message? "In times like these," "we're all in this together," or "we're here for you" were repeated over and over by different companies. One brand blurred together with the next. You have to dive deep to discover a complex organization's true capabilities and, from that, the sense of mission and purpose.

The Strategist knows it's there, and within that, they will find a beat, a syncopation, a rhythm to its component parts.

"A great leader must put the heartbeat in place if it's not there," says Mike Zawalski. And once there's a beat, "refine it, make it repeatable and predictable and consistent so all the constituencies that are a part of that organization are served by or are supplied by that organization know what to expect of it. That creates excellence and value."

Strategist leaders set the tone for the organization, and if mission and vision is of the first order, its foundation is built on culture, which synthesizes all the component parts within a complex organization to a steady pulse. "Every organization has a culture and I used to think, well, it just exists. It's just there. Not much you can do about it," describes Daniel Hamburger, CEO of Provation Medical and former CEO of Adtalem Global Education. "It turns out you can be intentional and shape the culture that you want and intentionally steer it in alignment with the strategy of the organization."

Barry Zekelman has seen other CEOs of large companies gloat that they won a new contract by cutting wages by $2 or $3 per hour. "They say we really beat them down, we won," but Zekelman feels sorry for them. "You won? Do you have any idea of the culture and environment you created? I mean, we're not a corporation, we're a culture. And when you create a culture of takeaway, how do you think they're running your shop? How do you think they feel about you caring for them?"

He shares that in thirty-four years he's never cut anyone's wages—not by so much as a penny. In the next breath he's quick to say he's not an employment agency, that they've had to work hard when plants are not up to snuff or making lean improvements. Zekelman Industries turns out 2.4 million tons of steel tubing from fifteen plants in the US and Canada, showing no signs of slowing down. He circles back to his superpower: the ability to give up control to get control, to empower teammates to have control of their own destiny.

An anonymous poet in Australia summed it up perfectly, writing, "We're all in the same storm. But we are not in the same boat." The world is what it is, but that doesn't dictate your circumstances or your organization. That's for you to determine.

The Strategist Leader

• Reliable	• Trustworthy	• Adaptable
• Decisive	• Strong	• Disciplined
• Empowering	• Accountable	• Mission driven
• Visionary	• Loyal	• Role model

In the Trenches
with Strategists

"A person who leads without followers
is just taking a walk."
—Christie Hefner

Strategists lead in high-pressure, high-visibility roles with increasing complexity. How do they best fight bureaucracy and MBA-speak while still growing an aligned organization? How do they straddle the competing needs of controlling the commanding heights, while still demonstrating to their troops the zeal of being able to jump into the trenches when necessary?

This section is a deeper dive into Strategists' winning habits. We look at how Strategists overcome obstacles and create powerful alignment and loyalty among large teams, in the hundreds, thousands, or tens of thousands—a synchronization that causes them to excel beyond peers, beyond competition. Finally, we take a look at what happens when power drives the leader sideways.

In running multibillion-dollar organizations, Susan Sentell says that whenever she was facing a tough time, her father repeated a question to ask of herself: If not me, then who? If the answer is that no one else can handle the situation any better than you can, then go forward, boldly. To succeed in complex and high-pressure environments, Strategists develop a toolkit to navigate and lead.

If cadence is one side of the Strategist's coin, alignment is the other, focusing on inspiring the organization to embrace and move toward common goals.

For Mhayse Samalya the first step in achieving alignment is, ironically, to reject any sense of homogeneity in the organization. He notes that all large teams can be divided into three tiers. First come high performers, some of whom can be coached to motivate others. Then he sees people at the bottom who are not performing and need to either leave the company or be reassigned to jobs that are a better fit. Finally, and most importantly, is the broad middle—people who have the closest touch to all the troops on the ground.

To make change, and make it stick, the key is uncovering the differences in motivation. The crucial understanding here is that motivations are not the same across all levels and groups. "Sometimes very high-performing people expect everyone to be high-performing and they expect everyone to work as hard as they do and they expect everyone to be motivated by the same things that they're motivated by," says Samalya. "Typically, very successful people are motivated by recognition, accomplishment, and money, and they have a tendency to assume everybody is motivated by that. They're not."

He gives an example of how mindsets differ: "Some people are motivated tremendously by having a day off, but a lot of people who are of high performance don't want a day off. They just want to keep coming to work every day. Every damn day," he says adding that the Strategist must figure out who is motivated by what, especially those in the middle of the pack—the portion that holds massive potential. "It's so big and if you can move that middle just a little bit—just incrementally—it has a multiplicative effect on the entire company."

THE ART OF ALIGNMENT

There is an art to aligning disparate elements around a common vision. "My meetings are run by questioning and intellectual curiosity and helping people explore and find common ground as opposed to directing, and dictating, and opinion giving," says one Fortune 500 CEO.

"Once everyone's heard, I felt like my role was to synthesize, or try to boil it down to something where people can again buy in even if it's a small degree," says Samalya. This chief synthesizer approach stands in contrast to the old autocratic style. He says if you simply order people around, "you can accomplish some things, but you haven't enrolled people. If you can bring people along, get people to buy in, you're going to end up with a much better result."

Christie Hefner, former Chairman and CEO of Playboy Enterprises, credits her background as a journalist for helping her pull out different viewpoints. "If I was chairing a meeting, I developed the habit—whether it was a board meeting or executive committee meeting—of calling on everyone in the room to speak to the issue instead of just the people who volunteered, and trying to get everybody in the room to speak to both the positives and the negatives of what was being considered. Not just to advocate one point of view or to hold back or to fall into the trap of trying to figure out what I thought we should do and then tell me that."

Former Best Buy President Shawn Score describes himself as inclusive and willing to test new ideas. He says, "I never made a major decision that had significant financial impact to the organization or people impact without involving more people than just myself and the executive team." Score always assumed that any plan built at the corporate level at Best Buy was 70 percent right.

"If we are onto something, we roll, and tweak along the way," he says. "I had groups across the country in various jobs who would meet, get on the phone regularly, and deal with the other 30 percent till we got the plan right."

In asking for outside opinions, Score didn't always like what he heard, but he found it critical in knowing how employees felt before executing something, even if quite sensitive. He could foresee issues that would pop up, if not in his region, then elsewhere. When someone raised an issue, Score says, "Generally, I would respond directly so they knew that the President of US stores was listening."

It was this engagement with employees that had a major impact. "They were actually part of the problem solving and solution, and when that happens, you've got automatic buy-in and credibility. You can say, 'Joe, our time guy in the warehouse, and Amy, a supervisor in IT, and Bill, a store manager in Fargo, North Dakota, were on this project team and here is how they fixed the problem,'" he says, adding that they often captured these stories on videos that were used to educate and motivate across the whole organization.

"I put a five-part video training session together around Best Buy Mobile so that everybody understood what we were trying to do because it was kind of a mystery and felt like we were doing something to the stores instead of the stores helping us do something," Score says.

CHEERLEADER-IN-CHIEF

ReSource Pro CEO Dan Epstein sees his job in the same way, empowering people within the organization, and like many smart Strategists, he fixates on inclusivity. "Whenever I would visit our operations in China, I would always think of myself not as the CEO, but the Cheerleader-in-Chief trying to help people understand how they fit into the broader picture. We were always trying to give people line of sight into the business strategy so that what they did had meaning for them."

When leadership of a company makes a decision, whether it's buying machinery or putting in safety equipment, Barry Zekelman thinks it can create anxiety among employees who might wonder why, what are you doing, and what does this mean for me? His take is this: "What's wrong with talking to them about it? All of those things relieve anxiety and build trust. And when you do that, you empower those teammates to become really part of your success."

In an interview with *Fortune*, Jim Sinegal, cofounder and CEO of Costco Wholesale, recalled working at age eighteen for Sol Price, founder of the discount retailer FedMart: "Sol spent day and night teaching us. He'd go home to have dinner, then come back to the warehouses. If he saw a piece of trash on the floor, he'd pick it up. If he noticed that a display was too high or an aisle wasn't wide enough, he'd fix it. As employees, we were tested every day, and if something wasn't done properly, he'd be certain to show us how to do it. Some people believe that you should say something just once. But I think you get a message across by communicating it every day. That's why I'm always walking the floors of different Costcos and talking to employees about the tasks at hand. It's not just because I love to hear the registers ring! Sol taught me that a good manager must also be a good teacher. A lot of very bright people lose sight of that."

Modeling behavior can be a huge determinant of morale, work ethic, and probability of great results. Quaker Oats veteran executive Mike Zawalski says, "I structure my day. I'm on time 99.9 percent of the time. I'm human and I may miss, but in a period of a hundred meetings, I'll be on time for ninety-nine. I expect other people to do the same and try to end on time."

Modeling the behavior Shan Atkins seeks did not go unnoticed when she began a job as a senior executive at Sears. A week into being hired Atkins sat in her first staff meeting where the head of merchandising—a legend in the apparel world—went around the table pointing at people to accompany him on the corporate jet and visit stores in Puerto Rico.

"I realized I would be missing Halloween, which was huge with my two boys, ages three and six. My family had just moved," remembers Atkins who said sorry, but she couldn't go on that date. It was the biggest day of the year after Christmas and birthdays for her family. "He just kind of looked at me very quizzically," she says. "Then he said, 'Okay, we'll do the trip the next week.' Afterward I was mobbed and thanked by other people in the room."

IT'S US TOGETHER

Having acquired a lot of companies, Barry Zekelman says the first thing he does when he buys a company or plant is go in and spend—up to a half million dollars—on the locker room and bathrooms. Why? "Because they're human beings and I want to treat them with respect and show them we care," he says. "If my wife or daughter can't go into the bathroom, then it's not good enough. People say this is different. This isn't us versus them. This is us together."

A mighty and enduring culture matched with emphasis on a cohesive team are the makings for an effective organization. Zekelman knows that a company is not always perfect, but he wants people to be happy at work. Talking to employees, he says, "I don't want you working sixty, seventy, eighty hours a week. That's failure to me." His goal is for people to have a family life and feel safe. Call it self-serving, but if they are working around the clock, with kids at home at loose ends, or prone to getting in trouble, employees will bring that back to work. Everyone loses.

Beyond setting a good example, the Strategist's ability to entrust and delegate not only creates alignment, but results. When Shawn

Score took over Best Buy as President of the mobile phone division, they held a mere one-half of 1 percent market share. In five years it had grown fourteen-fold against entrenched competition, to 7 percent market share, a number that he describes as "outrageous." Best Buy became the number three carrier, and Score credits what he calls a legion of advocates within the 130,000-person-strong company.

"I had a group of champions scattered all throughout the country," he says. "Every market and every role in the organization was represented." These individuals led the charge talking to employees, getting ideas, advocating in stores, and helping store managers adjust and make the changes necessary to differentiate themselves.

Fast growth was mirrored by the highest customer and employee satisfaction scores ever achieved by Best Buy. "There was a very clear mission with the inspection of each store to be certified as Renew Blue, meaning they understood and were executing the operating model," he says, explaining that they had a change management team ready at hand. "We called them inspections—once the store showed a proficiency of 95 percent, they were certified—but there were more coaching sessions."

Shawn Score's greatest passion was to spend days in Best Buy stores or district offices meeting with employees "instead of paying consultants to go do the work and find out what I should already know by talking to the employees." When he realized that over the years they had spent $100 million on consultants, enough was enough. "All they do is go into the store and do exactly what we're paid to do: observe, talk to the employees, figure out what's good, what's not working, and start to fix."

When Score took over, he had to change the cadence and communication in the stores. "Our job as regional managers, district managers, store managers is to openly communicate, address the top ten issues that are getting in the way," he says. They called these pain points and measured and addressed them with a system using red, yellow, and green.

"Within six months all the pain points had moved from red to green. It was that simple because, other than IT, these weren't complex problems. Nobody had just taken the time to do it. So instead of paying tens of millions of dollars a year to consultants, we stopped doing it, saved that money, and became our own consultants."

Jeff Chalovich saw firsthand the power of showing his workforce of 26,000 people that he was there for them. As he looked at the multibillion-dollar acquisitions they had made, it was impossible to avoid noticing the damage done to culture from trying to fit disparate organizations together. His solution was intensive and necessary if they were going to reset and restore a healthy culture. He set a goal to meet with all 2,600 supervisors in eighteen months, a big feat for one executive at a multibillion-dollar organization. Miraculously, he met his goal.

What took place when he visited a plant they'd acquired showed how that support affected the team. "They were all wearing union jerseys when I came in the plant, and I spent half a day on the floor with all of them talking and there was a lot of banter," Chalovich remembers. "But by the time their lunch came around, they went inside and put WestRock shirts on and took their union shirts off. Those things are what I'm most grateful for, whether it was on the shop floor or in the boardroom, people could relate to me and I could inspire them and build a great team and align a whole team on goals that we could reach together."

Getting the team in alignment propelled Chalovich to reach extraordinary milestones at WestRock. When he was given the mission to get their margin up from 12 percent to over 20 percent, he knew it was no small order. The competition was already doing far better in what the industry acknowledges is a commodity product. He describes his nine-year run, first as Executive Vice President, then as Chief Commercial Officer and President as dog years, having to shutter thirty-five of their 130 box plants, upgrade the Six Sigma team, get employee attrition down from 12 percent to 3 percent, move profit accountability from a plant level to a division level, switch out 40 percent of his top management team (ninety managers), and move from ten operating systems down to two to achieve their ultimate goal of increasing margin. His game plan and the actions he took to accomplish that goal illustrate how a Strategist leader must simultaneously move areas of a complex organization to get there.

A STOMACH FOR INTERNAL POLITICS

When trying to push change and improvement through a complex organization with lasagna-like layers of authority, personalities, opinions, and convictions, Strategists have to assume roles not present in smaller, more nimble organizations.

"In the Strategist role you've got to have the stomach for the politics of the situation," Mhayse Samalya acknowledges. Even black swan–type, cataclysmic leaps forward in innovation—a Facebook or Google—can become sclerotic, bogged down, and reactionary despite great product, mission, and quick market dominance. Google at twenty-three years old is still primarily one product: search. Search generated 86 percent of revenue in 2019 while employing 75,000 people. It is not the same lean, mean fighting machine it was on launch or IPO.

Some Strategists defend the value of bureaucracy in an organization at scale. "A certain amount of bureaucracy is important. It allows for consistency and reproducibility," says one senior executive who leads a division with 3,000 employees. "It allows for leverage where you can take your talent and not have them too focused on just the administrative side of what needs to be done each day."

Others seek to wage war on bureaucracy. Barry Zekelman is proud that even with close to 3,000 employees, his steel manufacturing company operates with very few foremen or supervisors. "They just slow things down. The only thing they are there for is a crutch," he says, adding that everyone who runs the equipment knows how to do it far better than he or anyone else ever would.

He focuses on empowering and trusting his team. "They know what to do. I ask them, would you ever get on an airplane or a bus not knowing if the pilot or driver is ready to go? Or not knowing your destination, what seat you're going to sit in, when we're going to stop, when we're going to turn. That's why we share the plan and communicate. They see the driver and they know the route. It reduces all the questions and anxiety."

ALL EYES ON FAILURE

Strategists confer authority on the team. They give their people agency and resources to work and make decisions on ways to improve products, services, and customer experience, and they encourage risk taking, knowing failures will happen.

Daniel Hamburger grew industrial supply giant W. W. Grainger's e-commerce unit from $10 million to $250 million. He then did the same for Adtalem (formerly called DeVry), growing the online division from $25 million to $250 million, ultimately heading up the entire organization with responsibility for $2 billion in revenue and 18,000 employees.

Despite Hamburger's great track record, the management team made a bad acquisition based on a faulty forecast. "It turned out to be a sector where there's basically only room for a number one and number two player. We were kind of a distant third," he remembers. In an attempt to recover, they tried to buy number two, but when they were outbid, they ended up selling to cut their losses. "It was not a good investment for us. It was definitely one of my worst days."

Some blunders are a lot more public, and a company's reaction can be a direct representation of the Strategist's style. In the middle of what could be a PR nightmare, owning the mistake or even using a little humor can be the saving grace.

In early 2018, a big chunk of Kentucky Fried Chicken's 900 stores in the United Kingdom closed their doors after running out of chicken. Social media had a field day, slamming the company, declaring a #KFCcrisis. Chicken lovers were outraged, just outraged. Many said they would take their cravings elsewhere. KFC had just switched to a new delivery contract that wasn't working as planned, but that was all just blah blah to hungry customers. Then came KFC's brilliant and public mea culpa, mea culpa, mea maxima culpa.

The company ran a full-page advertisement in the *London Evening Standard* with a photo of an empty chicken bucket, scattered crumbs, their logo now reading *FCK*. In an instant, the narrative changed. The fun and snarky apology led to even more buzz, and even a little bit of a PR legend. The team must have been channeling Colonel Sanders who once said: "One has to remember that every failure can be a stepping-stone to something better."

The definition of a new age of Strategist is one who seeks to be held accountable. "I started kicking myself out of my team meeting a couple times a year," says Daniel Hamburger. "I say, you guys talk about me, talk about whatever you want to talk about, how can we improve things. One person would take notes, anonymized. I got so much good feedback and ideas for how I could improve my style out of that, I call it the reverse executive session."

The best Strategists never stop learning. There is a continual process of self-discovery and reinvention. CEO Dan Epstein says, "When I joined the company, it took me eight months to make my first sale. I really didn't understand very much about insurance. I didn't understand the needs of our clients. I have to credit the board who gave me the space to go potentially fall on my face."

Under Epstein's leadership, the company has grown from twenty employees to 5,000, and he says, "I don't feel like I've accomplished very much yet. There's no sense of satisfaction or complacency. It's just a hunger to continue to build and grow and deliver great service."

Strategists are the lifeblood of complex and large organizations where their uncanny ability to create strong mission and vision drive continual advancement. Jamie Dimon at JPMorgan Chase, Fred Smith at FedEx, Satya Nadella at Microsoft, or Bob Iger at Disney exemplify how a leader and company can prove so enduring over such a long span of growth that investors, customers, and team continue to follow knowing they are in good hands.

We need more Barry Zekelmans, Janine Davidsons, and Mhayse Samalyas who will expend themselves over a lifetime to build, grow, maintain, rebuild, and scale the economic engines of growth. The most successful Strategists don't stand still, and they won't allow it.

A leader in the graphics, gaming, and AI space, NVIDIA's founder Jensen Huang puts it in this kind of alarmist way, telling his team: "We're always thirty days away from going out of business." Even with more than $10 billion in revenue, that's a sustaining hunger, an eagerness for the fight that is essential for a successful Strategist to lead at scale.

You Know You Are a Strategist If ...

✓ You operate at global scale, leading a complex or large organization.

✓ You sense and set the rhythm, the heartbeat of the organization across teams, divisions, functions, and board.

✓ You enjoy and excel at synthesizing various points of view.

✓ You coordinate and marshal people and resources.

✓ You are tuned into long-term vision.

✓ You know culture is critical and can be shaped.

✓ You turn structure into repeatable, defensible systems.

✓ You are passionate about developing and mentoring people.

✓ You have been functionally cross-trained over a span of years and through various roles.

✓ Your superpower is in setting vision and mission to drive a bigger strategy.

✓ You are wired to serve people and the organization.

✓ You are articulate, strong in communicating ideas and motivating others.

✓ You excel at managing teams, investors, boards, stakeholders, often with diverse agendas.

✓ You are adaptable to many different types of situations.

✓ You were mentored by inspiring predecessors.

5.

And Mighty Forces Will Come to Your Aid: Applying the FABS Styles to Your Organization

Leading is an exercise that shows itself only in action. It's in the guts, grit, and gumption of working with people and making decisions. It can be messy. It is never perfect or complete. It is physical as much as it is cerebral. Like riding a bicycle, leading is something you feel in your bones as much as in your head. It can start with sheer terror that evolves to trust and mastery, with balance only coming over time and with forward movement.

You discover how a leader performs and what makes them tick in the midst of planning, decision, execution, and aftermath. Fixers, Artists, Builders, and Strategists do not share the same wiring, but therein lies the opportunity for an organization to embrace the right leader in the right role at the right time.

We've covered each of the FABS leadership styles in the previous chapters, but to figure out what style of leader your company needs, when you need them, and in what role, division, project, client, or team, first we must cover what is true of leaders and organizations who embrace FABS leadership styles. Three principles—or qualities in a leader—serve to enhance an organization striving for better and best.

- Principle #1. Leaders Who Combine Strengths: Multiplying Force in a Changing and Evolving Organization
- Principle #2. Leaders Who Double Down: Reinforcing Highest and Best Use for Better Organizational Results
- Principle #3. Leaders Who Don't Hide: Increasing Accountability in Your Organization

FABS Principle #1: Leaders Who Combine Strengths

Multiplying Force in a Changing and Evolving Organization

"In nature, phase change takes a lot of energy," says expert Chief Operating Officer Mike Bartikoski. "If you think about water, going from water to ice or water to steam, the energy at phase change is highest. The phase change going from a twenty-five-person venture with tens of millions in sales to a hundred-person venture with hundreds of millions in sales, that requires a lot of energy and a very specific skill set to manage."

Successful organizations have mastered or perhaps simply weathered cycles of growth, turmoil, overhaul, and improvement. When a company is faced with dramatic change, the needs for leadership also can and will change. Leadership expert Adrienne Duffy points out: "There are times when leadership in any of these four modes might be required. At one juncture we may need a Fixer. But if we're fixing the way things *were* done and we're not innovating, we could fall into stagnation, in which case we need to get an Artist leader on the scene."

Fixers, Artists, Builders, and Strategists develop unique capabilities that can be tapped into at different points in the life of an organization. True FABS leaders recognize this need, see different strengths and modes as complementary, and intentionally apply them based on the specific needs of the organization.

Psychologist John Behr notes that a unique approach to work and leadership is what he calls spikiness. Picture a chart rating a range of individual qualities. The high points—the spiky points—are competencies and excellence above average. Dr. Behr explains, "If you have a team composed of eight people, for example, and every one of those team members has something spiky, but different, valuable, and relevant to that environment, then as long as the rest of their competencies do not derail them, you benefit from those eight spiky talents. That's optimal."

He explains, "The goal is to have at least one really spiky true expression that has value. If that leader's expression is powerful and spiky enough, then you can build around that." He drives home the value of that special contribution: "You really only need to be good at one or two things, and you can have an important place on the team. That's a dramatic way of building a team, shaping it with that intention."

Fixer CEO John Short explains it this way: "I use basketball as an analogy with my teams. If you think about a successful basketball team, you need a point guard, shooting guard, small forward, power forward, and center who all want to play together, but they have wildly different skill sets and physically they're all wildly different." When those unique abilities combine—each best in their own way—they make something far greater and more powerful as a collective whole.

Depending on the organization, FABS leadership modes are needed in different measures. CEO Lisa Yarnell observes that as difficult as it is to define a changing business segment, it's even more difficult to define the right person if they are not present within the leadership team. "If the times change, and the market changes, and the processes change, and the company thinks the team they groomed forever and ever and ever can do that, they're wrong," she says. "It's like a bad parent. You have to know that a teenager is different from a ten-year-old."

The issue, however, is that many organizations and leaders fail to do regular check-ins to see what is needed now. What has changed. Or what needs to change.

ASSESSING ROLES, ADDING TO THE TEAM

What if, when you see your doctor, they were to ask, "How are you feeling?" If your answer is, "Terrific. I ran a marathon ten years ago," that doesn't count. A lot happens in ten years. But in management circles it is common to hear a flashback to years prior such as, "Oh, they went to an Ivy League school," as an automatic qualifier for smarts, capability, or fitness for a role.

The marketplace pays no attention to pedigree or credentials where success is the acid test, not status. If we view roles and responsibilities through the lens of FABS leadership, it opens up an opportunity to embrace a leader based on what's missing, while taking advantage of the complementary strengths of the team.

Is the organization broken or bleeding? Call in a Fixer. Is the need to drive systems and teams essential for a large or complex organization? Add a Strategist. Has it been a long time since anyone shipped anything new? Bring on an Artist. Does the most promising new product or division seem poised for explosive growth, but no one's done it before? It's time for a Builder.

What type of leader is needed now in your organization? We see how complementary leadership styles can serve to reinforce each other, by looking at the process, approach, system, and style of Fixers, Artists, Builders, and Strategists. See comparison chart on page 191.

- **Process:** the steps taken to achieve a goal
- **Approach:** the method used in dealing with the challenge or opportunity
- **System:** the framework applied based on principles, mechanisms, or procedures
- **Style:** the manner in which a leader expresses their driving force

WINNING COMBINATIONS AT WORK

Peel back the layers of sales, marketing, finance, and operations that make up any organization that has achieved significant success, and at its heart there is a story of complementary leadership styles contributing mightily to the success of the business.

Legendary Intel CEO Andy Grove was reported to have said of Avram Miller, one of his lieutenants and the cofounder of Intel Capital (and to our way of thinking, an Artist leader): "You always needed a wild duck like Avram, a nonlinear thinker that stirred up the others. I always try to have an Avram on my team. Always. They disrupt and create."

Artist leaders like Miller can be found in organizations big and small. He sees loyalty and support of diverse talents on the team as a two-way street, saying that while he pioneered groundbreaking developments, he couldn't have done it without Intel. Psychologist John Behr notes: "The head of the organization doesn't need to be an innovator. They just have to be willing to drive and support and embrace innovation."

Strategist and CEO of Gateway Foundation, Tom Britton, experienced this firsthand. "I hired an Artist very intentionally because she is brilliant," he says. "I can do it, but it's not my first strength. I hired her to fill a gap and she has just killed it. A huge success." Leaders must have a self-awareness about their own strengths to challenge the status quo.

Process	Approach	System	Style
Fixer			
Turnaround What is Broken or Bleeding. Laser focus 24/7 on reviving the most damaged companies, divisions, products, services.	**Lone Ranger.** Rallies the core team, but does what is necessary to turn things around even if isolating and isolated.	**Controls.** The Fixer deals with mess by putting controls in place.	**Velocity.** Speed is life; stagnation is death.
Artist			
Infuse New Thinking. Focus on delivering the creative spark, capable of leaps in product and service offerings.	**Outsider Perspective.** This renegade brings the unique, outsider, unseen, and overlooked perspective needed to advance, jump, pivot, reverse, and double back.	**Production.** The Artist transforms chaos into new product, measured for success against which to be successful must be produced and tested in the marketplace.	**Creation.** The new, the reinvented, anything to create, to envision, to re-envision.
Builder			
Achieve Explosive Growth. Relentless focus on dominating new markets, products, and taking companies to scale. One after another.	**Team Leader.** To grow products and services, the Builder puts process and team in place to expand and leverage capabilities.	**Structure.** Builders put structure and process in place, setting the stage for and in anticipation of rapid growth.	**The Market.** Satisfying customer needs and taking companies to the next level and new markets.
Strategist			
Move through a Complex Organization. Tackle incessant demands night and day to move between teams, divisions, stakeholders, communities.	**Quarterback.** First among equals but really the ultimate team player, they live for the team. Sees the entire field and how all elements combine for success and align against the common enemy.	**Systems.** Strategists hone repeatable systems that cause large and complex organizations to scale ever greater heights. Moving the vast middle: together, faster.	**Cadence.** Measuring and quickening the pulse and beat of the organization and its parts, setting the direction and coordinating the pace to achieve ambitious goals.

Organizational design expert Bernie Liebowitz describes how a Strategist can align with an Artist: "The Strategist has to be willing to change, and one of the things that is going to cause the changes are the challenges from the Artist types that are on their payroll. Many times, Artist leaders come up with new ideas and often times it's a challenge to the old way of doing things. Strategists recognize that. They recognize that they themselves are not the Artist type, or even if they come up with good ideas, they're always looking for someone who sees the world beyond the immediate, and many times the successful ones find it."

CEO Russ Reeder gives an example of a Builder helping a company deliver a product in a scalable way, then handing off to a Strategist and team that will expand resellers, channels, and markets. Is the Strategist the end point once an organization reaches global size? Reeder says no. Other leadership modes must be infused to encourage the organization to keep busting through future ceilings. "If they are not trying to figure out where are our customers changing, what's our competition making, what products are needed—then they just go into maintenance mode."

MASTERING INFLECTION POINTS

Over the life of an organization, there is continual movement that becomes cyclical, from growth to retrenchment to renewal to metamorphosis. Significant points of change or inflection points in an organization can each call for different or additional FABS modes, and the resulting collaboration is a synthesis and coordination among complementary talents.

Artist leader Andy Crestodina recalls the moment at his web development shop, Orbit Media Studios, when he had had enough. "As Orbit grew, there was an obvious need for greater skills in management, which I have no background in and totally lack," he says, recognizing that though he owned and controlled the company, he was part of the problem.

"I'm not at all a CEO. It is a beautiful thing to see it done well. I was in a role where I was limiting the growth of Orbit and I knew it." He had a second problem alongside the challenge of not excelling as CEO: "I was doing almost all of the sales myself trying to support a team of twenty-two. I'd spend all day on phone calls and in meetings. I'd spend all night writing proposals. It was totally unsustainable."

Something had to give.

Luckily Crestodina had an ace in the hole, which was his willingness to put his ego aside matched with an eagerness to share both power and rewards. You've heard the expression, when the student is ready, the teacher will appear, and in his case, that's exactly what happened: the right person showed up. One of his customers, Todd Gettelfinger, could see the company was struggling and offered to help, first in planning, then in taking a hands-on approach to make the plan a reality. Skilled in operations, Gettelfinger started by hiring a sales team, then launched a client services group to take on strategy projects for clients. It proved to be the winning combination that made Orbit, well, achieve orbit and become a sustainable business with hundreds of clients.

Crestodina recalls: "Not long after our CEO joined us, I suddenly had twenty hours a week of extra time, and when I drove that time and effort into content marketing and thought leadership, I was able to create an annual conference, write a book, and create a monthly event. I doubled my publishing frequency. If I hadn't redefined my role, you wouldn't be talking to me now. I would just be a burned-out website salesman had I not found and recruited Todd for the CEO role. He saved us."

Today Crestodina has moved to global prominence as one of the foremost recognized experts in search engine optimization and online content marketing. By obsoleting himself from the CEO role, hiring a Builder, and becoming the new Chief Creative Officer, he orchestrated a remarkable result. He didn't relinquish ownership. He didn't retire and he didn't delegate. He collaborated radically to both double his company's size and focus on what he did best.

Andy Crestodina's journey as company owner and lone ranger to a leader much more focused on sharing responsibility and staying within his core strength is not impossible. Ryan Landry, President of New Horizons Learning Group, a chain of technology and leadership training facilities in the western US, recalls the moment he broke down. "We were at a company strategy session with the whole management team present, and I just lost it," he says.

Running the franchise owned by his family, Landry had managed through crisis after crisis, putting out fire after fire, even though his growing capability as a leader was much more expressive as Builder and Artist. The needs of the organization demanded he do what was necessary, but the Fixer role was not only energy draining, it was destroying his joy for work and distancing him from his family. He says the breakthrough about showing his pain caused a radical reenergizing from his management team to move him from Fixer to Builder mode. It takes a measure of authenticity to put ego aside, even if just a bit, to think about what the organization needs, and what can be leveraged by each person on the team.

David Ormesher had a similar realization as he grew his company, closerlook. He sought to create a leadership team that could operate without his daily intervention, enabling him to double down on his own strengths and build a much bigger future. "There was a time when I touched everything. You're always hands-on when you're building, but I know a lot of my peers who are running companies like mine that are two, three times our size and they're still in the minutiae of hands-on," Ormesher says. "Nothing leaves their shop without them reviewing it, and I just look at them and ask why. It's principally because they're afraid. They don't trust their people or they're afraid to give it up."

He resolved not to keep himself in the same siloed, static position as his competitors. He removed himself from day-to-day management of the team's 200 employees for a more visionary role, but it was not without pain: "I went through a period of about a year when I felt lost. I questioned my meaning, like, why am I here? I used to draw my meaning because I could look at the end of the day and say I created this, I wrote that, I envisioned this and now I can't do that anymore. I began to realize that I have a different role to play: to build, and support, and motivate, and challenge my team so that they can go and do it even better than I. That's success."

ONE SIZE DOES NOT FIT ALL

As appreciation for your highly unique way of leading grows, it becomes easier to reject and discard that which is not for your highest and best use, and intentionally seek out resources based on gaps to be filled. The identical can be said for company owners, boards of directors, and investors who have a view of the playing field and can take an active role in identifying which FABS leadership style needs to be brought to bear.

For leaders, choosing and rejecting opportunities is not easy, especially if your perception of the world is scarcity. Not enough prospects, roles, income, or power. Not enough kudos, acknowledgment, praise, or recognition. Not enough love or respect. If you think there's just not enough opportunity to lead—if your framework doesn't have abundance as part of your mindset—it's easy to doubt your gift and grab for whatever might work.

TIGER 21's Michael Sonnenfeldt recalls an executive he brought on board who did well—until he didn't. "I invested where the CEO was an amazing Fixer," he says. As the executive continued to excel at fixing, Sonnenfeldt thought he was amazing. But as the company got better, the executive got worse: "Growing the company could only come from investing in R&D and building up. All of a sudden he didn't look as strong as the magnificent performance he had given while fixing."

One size does not fit all. Not in shoes, not in love, not in leadership.

None of us do it alone. Collaboration sounds so obvious. But it does not maintain itself. It requires concerted effort among leaders and team, divisions, and departments.

Even a well-established company like Boeing, which just celebrated its 105th birthday, could be in need of a shake-up. All that experience making the best airplanes in the world (they are the largest US exporter) and yet they hit the worst of disasters with two deadly crashes of the 737 MAX, first in 2018 and then again in 2019.

When they then lost a missile defense contract in 2021, aviation industry expert Richard Aboulafia noted, "Boeing needs . . . to rethink where engineers fit in the company org chart. They need to rethink who runs the show. It's really shocking to have an engineering company that basically doesn't have engineers on its board. Boeing needs to empower engineers within the chain of command, reinforce engineering capabilities, and add more engineers to the board and leadership team."

Great leaders embrace bringing others on board who are better equipped for different parts of the journey. Organizational psychologist John Behr defines leadership as "the ability to know, perceive, and respond to your constituency or your team—the people around you—and to encourage focus, direction, and productivity."

"I've built a couple billion-dollar businesses from scratch, but I would have no competence to run them," says Michael Sonnenfeldt who credits his team with catapulting his real estate company quickly into the ranks of the top 100 developers in the US.

The average leader advances self against others. Successful leaders face the paradox of elevating their own career and abilities while *also* empowering the team by enhancing the skills and confidence of those around them.

Verinder Syal recalls a moment of realization: "When I was ten years into Quaker Oats, I was the youngest Vice President, head of strategy, and everyone's saying I'm great. I was working one weekend because I didn't think my team's work was satisfactory. A mentor stopped by and asked me what I thought my job was. And I had an epiphany. I thought my job was to put out the best product even if I had to do it myself. Thanks to this mentor I made a huge swing where my job became twofold. First, to make my people better than they ever could be. And also to put out a great product."

SURVIVAL OF THE COOPERATIVE

Some species of termites are unstoppable mound builders. They form the tallest structures on earth relative to their size. Compared to human-designed skyscrapers, termite mounds go vertical twice as high, termite for termite. The oldest mounds have been carbon dated back 3,800 years, perhaps dating back 7,000 years. There is no skyscraper built by man that could last a tenth as long. But the greatest thing about termite builders, the crowning glory, is that for all that construction expertise, there is no termite leader. There is no boss termite directing plans and execution. The only thing determining termite construction is proximity and function: what needs to be done gets done in the moment.

Darwin got it wrong. It was not really survival of the fittest that was being observed. It is survival of the cooperative.

In forest ecology, it was assumed trees of all species are engaged in a fight for sunlight. That thinking has been upended—a complete shift in the paradigm of competition—with new findings that trees communicate with both same and different species via vast fungal connective networks that allow communication, support, and supplies to be sent where needed in times of stress, drought, and disease.

Intense collaboration changes the game for how organizations view roles to be filled. No longer is a static title a complete description. Nor should a leader be confined to a box, riveted on one title, industry, or specialty. A richer understanding comes to the team from knowing someone's primary style of leadership—how they will jump into action—whether Fixer, Artist, Builder, or Strategist, leading to a greater degree of harmony.

FABS Principle #2:
Leaders Who Double Down
Reinforcing Highest and Best Use for Better Organizational Results

Diana Fongheiser owns one of the fastest growing pediatric therapy companies in the US. When we met her years ago, her army of 400 occupational therapists, physical therapists, speech therapists, and social workers was deployed throughout the Philadelphia school system, providing the gold standard in care for 200,000 students. Big plans were brewing and Fongheiser had her eye on expansion by acquiring a number of providers in other states.

There was just one problem. In her gut she knew that her legacy management team wouldn't cut it. She needed different and more expert skill sets to expand their current business and take charge integrating acquisitions. So she made a move to systematically replace people in favor of more expert leadership.

By the time they made their biggest acquisition, which increased the team to 600 therapists in multiple states, she had a completely upgraded management team. Then COVID hit, closing schools worldwide. Every school her team served shut their doors, and within a day 100 percent of their workforce saw their work come to a screeching halt. How would the new team respond?

As luck would have it, she was now perfectly positioned, because the new team was wired for challenge and eager to prove themselves.

They immediately set about to shift to telehealth and remote treatment. The schools responded enthusiastically, and care rapidly went back up to close to normal standards.

Collaboration is the fertile ground in which an organization grows and thrives, and it requires leaders who are both accretive and distinct. The leader must be measurably accretive to the team, meaning that they actually have an expertise that is needed and valuable. And it must be a distinct competence.

Accretive is an exacting word in business, not fluffy or vague. In acquiring another company, for example, accretive means the combination adds more profits to the combined enterprise. Stripe executive Rob McClung applies the term rigorously even to the people on his team: "If you're not accretive to an organization that's single-minded, you're useless. How do you become accretive to what they do? That's the success story."

Too many leaders try to be all things to all people, trying to fit themselves into a role, no matter how ill fitting. To be accretive, the right leadership mode and strength must be brought to bear at the best points in the organization's life cycle or makeup. For many leaders, however, it can be a hard pill to swallow that a given role is not their highest and best use. And it's no easier for organizations or teams to navigate when it becomes apparent that what is needed, right now, might be something different.

CONTINUAL RE-CREATION AS A FORCE MULTIPLIER

A great leader is curious, nimble, and innovative, while also having a willingness to engage in the practice of self re-creation. You've no doubt noticed that FABS leadership styles have a degree of, shall we say, situational self-obsolescence. It's not actual obsolescence but more a personal form of creative destruction leading to re-creation, further strengthening their highest and best mode.

- **The Fixer** is wired to mend what's broken, then move on.
- **The Builder** is wired to grow the team, establish systems, dominate a market, and then move on to new markets, new products, new needs.
- **The Artist** is wired to see through fresh eyes, create, ship, experience market success, and then move to a new, fresh canvas.
- **The Strategist** is wired to move both laterally and in increasing responsibility and authority through different divisions, geographies, roles, and challenges within one or more complex organizations.

For FABS leaders, self-obsolescence in a completed project, client, or team role is matched by continual re-creation, increasing their effectiveness and more easily producing better results.

The situation and circumstance of the work changes. That's a given. And the successful leader doubles down by continually reinforcing their growth in experience and accomplishment (accomplishment meaning both positive and negative outcomes) resulting in deeper and deeper competence, better and better organization results. This is at the heart of Eric Kish fixing Petromidia, John Wu's algorithms at Travelmath, Russ Reeder's success growing Media Temple, and Carol Bernick's piloting of Alberto-Culver.

Re-creation happens individually, and also at the level of the successfully renewing organization.

This is not always comfortable ground. Former Vanguard Investments CEO Bill McNabb has publicly described the company's $1 billion process to create a new online offering at Vanguard.com as one meant to "essentially destroy themselves." It was a corporate bet not to incrementally improve but to fundamentally re-create the business. So, too, for the leader.

Winning performance in business can be nuanced, or it can take dramatic and bold acts of leadership to succeed. We applaud ingenious companies like Netflix and Vanguard, while glossing over the degree to which their acts of self re-creation and change can take them to the edge of failure. Netflix distributed DVDs by the millions, supplanting the brick-and-mortar retailer Blockbuster. But it was still a physical form of distribution. The company took a leap to the completely unknown idea of streaming. Building storage and streaming capability cost $40 million in hard cash. As costs increased and the market was still emerging, the stock plummeted from $42 to $10.

Netflix looks genius now—rulers of the streaming world—but only at the extreme cost of reinvention. There was no hiding. It was either move boldly, overtly, and decisively or prepare to be steamrollered by the next upstart.

YOUR JOB MAY NOT EXIST TOMORROW

Prior to joining Stripe, Rob McClung led a large team of Googlers in over a dozen global offices with hundreds of vendor agents supporting many languages. "I think some of the crazy things I accomplished, which could have undermined my job—and totally outside my job description—are also the things that got me promoted at Google, because you realize that your job today will not exist in about eighteen months," he says, pointing to his experience in the start-up world as giving him the scrappiness to thrive in that environment.

Google is an organization that defines itself by reinvention, by an ethos of constantly making processes (and thus entire divisions and teams) more efficient, more automated, perhaps redundant or obsolesced, causing managers and teams to not become entrenched, but instead to be nimble and confident in the face of an ambiguous future. They may in fact be working to eliminate their own function.

The modern form of the corporation remains strong because it works. But it is a construct that originated at the dawn of the industrial age, with strict top-down hierarchy. Rigid hierarchy is no longer the only or best solution. Rather, a flat, transparent, and collaborative environment is seen in most industries where breakthrough product is created and grown, in many cases by someone very junior in the organization. As machine learning becomes widespread, the legacy corporate model will be further strained, because it is based on a singular idea that the higher up you go in the organization, the more knowledge-intense, decision-making–capable you become.

McClung moved into a new leadership role in a new area of the business four times over the seven years he spent at Google. He says, "The same organization has 30 percent less Googlers but the impact each one is having is so much bigger. The volume of work increases, as does automation."

Automation is a pervasive theme. "You're trying to think about ways to again put yourself out of a job. You have to be comfortable with that. If you don't start with that scrappy mentality you see in the start-up world—if you're looking at incremental—it's not going to work," says McClung.

Award-winning architect, author, and AI researcher Randy Deutsch decided to model his career on seven-year cycles. His reasoning is practical. He believes that in every work experience, there are always two inflection points: the first, where you need to feel the subtle indicators that have changed in your industry, your company, or the world at large; and the second inflection point, when you get hit over the head by a proven reality. He graphed out these cycles for his career:

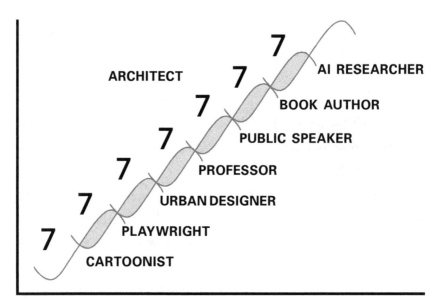

Architect and AI researcher Randy Deutsch's career graph in seven-year cycles.
© Deutsch Insights, 2021.

In architecture there have been repeat cataclysms and body blows to the profession inflicted by various events such as the introduction of computer-aided design, the Great Recession wiping out construction projects, and the pandemic putting projects such as restaurants and commercial office space on hold. These events may or may not have had tea leaves you could have read in advance, but Deutsch's point is, no matter what, there are going to be cyclical patterns in any career, industry, or long-term project.

Deutsch prides himself on being more and more tuned in to his world: "I view my entire career as an experiment, and I just decided to sacrifice myself throughout my career." He still calls himself an architect, and his cycles include professor, author of six books, speaker, and now NIH AI researcher. He doesn't even think his path is perilous: "I'm actually really risk averse. I've never owned a stock, only index funds. I redefine it as having intestinal fortitude. I don't like bungee jumping. But if I did, this is my version of bungee jumping."

PROJECT-BASED ROLES ENHANCE ORGANIZATION STRENGTH

The idea of a linear career path is disappearing, as more individuals take power into their own hands to seek new experiences and development rather than rely on one company to provide it. This project-based mentality has infiltrated much of the workplace. The management team at LinkedIn, for example, recognizes that employees will not spend their lifetime at LinkedIn or at any other single organization. Founder Reid Hoffman calls it a tour of duty, where at the end of a set time in one position, a person can advance to a new role within the company or look outside and elsewhere.

At the dawn of moviemaking, actors, directors, producers, and others were chained to studios by long-term, unbreakable contracts, but, over time, the model mostly broke. A new and different free-agent model took center stage, and as a result the *right* stars, screenplays, studios, and directors paired up to make a movie happen. Once the star or director completed the project, they moved on, but the quality of movies and freedom to do what each individual did best skyrocketed.

"I'm getting good parts. But the reason I love working is the crew," actress Shirley MacLaine told the *New York Times*. The star of classics including *The Apartment* and *Terms of Endearment* says, "That's a mini-civilization, with different points of view and attitudes toward work and time. Blue collar, white collar, no collar, money, critics, out-of-control emotionalism. All this goes on, and every bit of it is respected on set. I don't care who the idiot control-freak director is or isn't. We can't do it without one another. Have I got an example for a successful civilization? A movie set."

The free-agent model rules in many professions that operate by way of self re-creation. The actress makes her debut on the big screen, then moves on to the next career-advancing role. Your doctor's goal is to heal you, not keep you sick. The plumber shows up to fix the leak, then leaves. Expertise is rewarded.

While much of work is becoming project-oriented, this is not an argument for free agency for all. Careers for Fixers, Artists, Builders, and Strategists need not be nomadic, but they need to play to their strengths for the betterment of their companies, clients, and teams. There is no better way to enrich and enhance your career than to produce superior results for the stakeholders you answer to.

The wonders of continually diving deeper into your own well of excellence can be found in every career, every calling. Baseball Hall of Famer Cal Ripken said, "I made a ton of errors at shortstop during my first season. In '79 I moved to the Miami Orioles, a Class A team, but my problem with errors at shortstop started all over again. Lance Nichols, the manager, moved me to third base, and from then on everything clicked."

Let's unpack this a bit, because your coauthors are not exactly experts in baseball, but if we're hearing Ripken correctly, he stayed in the infield, and moved just one click over, as it were, about forty feet from shortstop—where he had failed—to third base, where he excelled.

What about you: in your organization, is everyone in their best role? If you manage others, is there any change, even slight, in positions or roles of the people on your team that could improve your game play? And in your role in your company, whether you manage others or just yourself, are you at shortstop or third base? Is there perhaps a one-click move that could serve you and the organization better?

Your move need not be inevitable or set forever in stone. As it turned out for "Iron Man" Cal Ripken, he proved to be not only a great third baseman for the Baltimore Orioles during his twenty-one seasons, but also one of the best shortstops the game has ever seen. His career improved, thanks to movement, not stasis.

As an organization grows, evolves, changes, paying attention to whether people should be shifted in their roles and responsibilities to play to their unique strengths can lead to a happier, more satisfied workforce, plus an increase in productivity and energy. Sometimes organizations hit a wall finding they don't have the right (or enough) resources internally to tackle big projects or challenges, so infusing a fresh perspective with an outsider or project-based leader can be just the ticket to start moving in the right direction.

EVERY FIBER OF YOU, COMMITTED

We see the best leaders committed to both excellence for themselves and commitment to their team. This full-on engagement shows up in a sacrifice, a desire to mentor and be mentored, a loyalty to those around them. Just watch skateboarders at a skatepark to understand all-in committed, no going back. When a skateboarder "drops in," they stand at the edge of the bowl with their back foot anchoring the board on terra firma, then stomp down on the front edge of the skateboard, which is hanging out over the bowl, and make a complete drop into nothingness, hoping the board will stay under their feet.

This move requires 100 percent commitment of every fiber of the skateboarder to dive headfirst into thin air. To land smoothly and glide forward at the base of the bowl and not face-plant, not even a 90 percent or even 99 percent effort will do it. Full commitment.

Michael Apted was a documentary filmmaker fresh out of college in 1963 when he was recruited to help produce a film called *Seven*

Up, which followed a group of fourteen seven-year-old students in England. Seven years later there was a sequel called *7 Plus Seven* following the same students, now age fourteen. Fast-forward to *63 Up*, aired in 2019, the ninth installment in the series, and the final year of Apted's remarkable life and career.

Who stays with something for fifty-six years? He continued to track their growth, victories, and tragedies decade on decade. He doubled down, and then again, and again. Film critic Andrew Sarris called the series "the most remarkable nonfiction film project in the history of the medium." Roger Ebert called it "the noblest project in cinema history."

Developing a deep understanding, appreciation, and acceptance of your best strengths—your highest and best use in the world—and then committing to an organization or team, applying that at the right time and place—takes reflection. Most leaders we interviewed say they are a mix, a combination of styles, but the most insightful can identify their dominant style and see what is not for their highest and best use, where they should decline, delegate, defer, reject.

As author and minister Jack Boland was fond of saying, just because you have a song to sing doesn't mean you don't have to learn how to sing it.

FABS Principle #3:
Leaders Who Don't Hide
Increasing Accountability
in your Organization

When Wells Fargo CEO John Stumpf was called to testify in a 2016 US Senate committee hearing investigating the bank's setting up of millions of unauthorized bank accounts, the bank's recorded quarterly earnings calls came under scrutiny. Senators noted that Stumpf had consistently, over the course of many quarters, trumpeted a key measure of the bank's progress: its increase in cross-selling of multiple products to existing customers. Quarter after quarter, nonstop revenue growth. But it turns out the cross-selling was a sham.

Employees had set up millions of accounts and charged fees without consent from account holders. Stumpf professed ignorance and could only repeat that decisions were not his as CEO but up to the board. That's hiding. Right out in the open. Not surprisingly, Stumpf was fired and then barred by the federal government from ever again working in the banking industry.

Leaders who avoid and hide from decisions, responsibility, and accountability can have tragic consequences across the organization and broader community. Wildfires have repeatedly devastated hundreds of thousands of acres in California, but the 2018 Camp Fire that sparked in the town of Paradise was the deadliest in California history, destroying 14,000 homes and killing eighty-five people. Among a number of causes, Pacific Gas & Electric's faulty equipment and lax safety practices were implicated for this fire and others in years prior. NBC reported that "a regulatory audit of the transmission system where the Camp Fire broke out found the company was late in fixing 900 problems on its towers and other equipment, including two critical threats that regulators say languished more than 600 days before being repaired."

California Governor Gavin Newsom summed it up: "They have simply been caught red-handed over and over again, lying, manipulating, or misleading the public. They cannot be trusted."

In 2020, PG&E was charged with involuntary manslaughter for the Camp Fire and pled guilty to eighty-four counts. The utility radiated and oozed years of terrible leadership, which begs the question: what if a leader had shown up who simply refused to ignore or go along with problems, who refused to hide? Time will tell if the company can turn around with the help of the new CEO, Patti Poppe, who intends to spend billions to put 10,000 miles of power lines underground.

David Ormesher, CEO of closerlook and founder of the Bigger Future project in Rwanda, says, "The core of leadership is authenticity and being able to look someone in the eye and make a claim and know in your deepest heart of hearts that the claim you're making is true."

Gaye van den Hombergh, leadership expert and former CEO, reflects on coaching some of the most successful Fortune 500 management teams: "When you look at the numbers—what organizations spend on leadership development, and how spending has been increasing over the years—the fact is that leadership quality has not improved. I see the opposite; the quality has gone down. There is a lack of vision, let alone an inspiring vision; a lack of holding people accountable. There is a fear of giving anyone constructive feedback. The things you would expect from top leaders—I don't see nearly enough of that."

"So many leaders of the largest companies, and in some cases government, do the wrong thing. They know it's wrong," says Glen Tullman, who has led fast-growing healthcare companies Allscripts, Livongo, and now Transcarent. He sees the biggest enemy being a lack of leadership. "I think we need real leaders who are refocused on what's important—on individuals, on our communities, on doing the right thing." He likes to quote Ashleigh Brilliant, a philosopher, who said, "Why don't we get braver as we get older?" Why don't we do the right thing, take more risks, invest in bold ideas?

ACCOUNTABILITY IN THE FACE OF CHAOS

Leadership, as we've observed, is an aspirational game: we look up to great leaders, we can easily spot the differences between winners and losers, and in increasingly transparent environments it's hard to both hide *and* produce results. Effective FABS leaders achieve superior results for owners, management, investors, and teams because they do not hide from making decisions, from engagement with their stakeholders, or from being held accountable for achieving goals.

Great leaders just *do.* Michael Sonnenfeldt of TIGER 21 recalls an early learning experience: "I once told my father I was working on a business and was so frustrated because the idea was fabulous, but the people were getting in the way, and my father basically said, lovingly, 'You're such an idiot. Ideas are a dime a dozen. The problem is rarely in the idea. It's always in the execution.' Leaders can be fooled by what I'll call the majesty of the idea and get lost in the execution. It's all about execution."

An experienced marathon runner told us the secret to his success. He said, leave it all on the field. What did he mean? Don't hold back. Don't end the game feeling like you still have gas in the tank. Don't play it safe. Don't cross the finish line feeling like you could have done more. And own the result—the great, the good, the mediocre, the bad.

Like a winning athlete, when you see a leader who excels far beyond the ordinary, it's never a halfway thing.

"All is chaos," says Chief Technology Officer David Mitchelhill, who has served in technology leadership roles in both corporations and government. Heading up the United Kingdom Criminal Justice System's £3.2 billion data integration project, he notes, "The simple thing is that anything we do, any form of work anywhere in the world is surrounded by change. Nothing is immutable. So you have a thousand connections to different things and every one of them is in change. Technology's in change, the business is in change, the world is in change, and therefore you have to accept that chaos. And if you don't accept that chaos and the ability to assimilate chaos, and deal with it, then you're going to fail."

Real estate broker and innovator Chris McAllister says leadership goes beyond IQ and EQ (emotional intelligence). "I think the biggest thing is your adversity quotient," he says. There is no shortage of challenges, often starting with the tendency in most organizations to doggedly hang onto the status quo, fiercely resisting any real change.

Successful leaders become defined by the biggest or seemingly impossible challenges. Chief Operating Officer Mike Bartikoski says, "The soft stuff *is* the hard stuff. It takes a lot of time to encourage the right sort of reporting structures, the right sort of dialogue, the right sort of coaching and platforms within a company to get to better execution."

We see a continual striving in great leaders. Arriving, and not yet arrived.

LEADERSHIP MAKES ALL THE DIFFERENCE

In smaller organizations the difference between great leadership and just so-so is the difference between life or death. Only 50 percent of small businesses with employees will make it to their fifth anniversary. By the tenth year, 30 percent will still be around.

Nobody gets a free pass. No leadership team is immune regardless of pedigree or past results. In the 1970s, the bluest of the blue chip public companies were the Nifty 50, including Kodak, Kresge, Sears, DEC, Emery, Schlitz, and Polaroid. All considered incredibly safe and yet seemingly offering the surest long-term returns. All now gone or a shadow of what they once were.

In the Olympics, the most decorated Olympian of all time is swimmer Michael Phelps, with twenty-eight medals, including twenty-three gold medals. Take just one of his races, the 2012 100-meter butterfly. The difference between his gold medal finish and fourth place was six-tenths of a second. Less than one second between victory and go home.

Leadership is science and art, especially in the sense that ambitious leaders work at improvement for better quality, speed, efficiency, functionality, cost, team cohesion, all aimed at better results. Adtalem's former CEO Daniel Hamburger says, "You can never move fast enough." Chief Technology Officer Griffin Caprio says, "Improving the team is never-ending and constantly changing in terms of the types of challenges you get to solve."

The leader as change agent is therefore in a constant state of movement. "Order is not enough," says author and psychologist Jordan B. Peterson in *12 Rules for Life: An Antidote to Chaos.* "You can't just be stable and secure and unchanging, because there are still vital and important new things to be learned." There is a point of balance, as he notes, "You need to put one foot in what you have mastered and understood, and the other in what you are currently exploring and mastering. Then you have positioned yourself where the terror of existence is under control, and you are secure, but where you are also alert and engaged."

6.

Seek Your Highest and Best Use

Dane Miller was bored.

The founder and CEO of medical device maker Biomet was sitting in his plant in Warsaw, Indiana. The power was out due to a record-breaking number of tornadoes that had knocked out the entire electrical grid in northern Indiana. Repairs were going to take a solid week and operations were on hold, so Miller phoned a surgeon friend and told him he was coming over. He wanted his buddy to slice open his forearm and tuck in a dime-sized slug of titanium.

Miller didn't need surgery. He had something he desperately wanted to prove. The nascent industry of hip and knee replacement was convinced stainless steel was the best material for implants, but Dane Miller thought differently. His prediction was that steel would eventually react and corrode inside the human body, while titanium would be impervious. No one believed him.

Even though his surgeon friend objected, the doctor stitched the titanium into Miller's forearm, and Miller left it there for ten years. Time and science proved Miller right, and titanium is now the industry standard for artificial hips and knees.

Miller described his leadership journey to us in 2009 in his Warsaw, Indiana, office. He handed over a framed front-page story *USA Today* had run on the newspaper's twenty-fifth anniversary that listed the best-performing companies over the same twenty-five-year period. Biomet was high on the list, having grown a colossal 30,000 percent to become a $12 billion med device leader, before eventually merging to become Zimmer Biomet.

Dane Miller came to know his highest and best use, and it informed his course from humble beginnings selling arm slings to doctors all the way up to the commanding heights of his industry. Even in his later years, he was known to drive the shuttle bus around the corporate campus or pick up job candidates at the airport to get an unvarnished, fresh view into areas of new opportunity.

Miller was unwilling to just sit still. He possessed a relentlessness to be his most ferocious self and to lead in a way that was an authentic expression of himself, damn the costs.

YOUR HIGHEST AND BEST USE

Robert Murray, an expert in behavioral science and business management, says that only about 5 to 10 percent of us have a genetic predisposition to become leaders. "This doesn't mean that they will either become leaders or become good leaders if they do," he says. "They may be driven to lead, but good leadership is learned." According to Gallup and other researchers, about 90 percent of leaders are in the *wrong* job. And when it comes to sustained growth, 86 out of 100 leaders fail.

Good steel must be tempered to be useful. Same with glass. It's brittle until it has been tempered at high heat. Rubber is only useful once it's been vulcanized. What about leaders? They also require heat and pressure of a sort, tempering and vulcanizing to become resilient.

Bildungsroman translates into English as a coming-of-age story but really means the possibility of finding one's authentic self. FABS leadership calls for *bildungsroman*, an authentic rise in excellence in your craft, seeking out roles that are a reflection of your true self in your best style and mode.

What is your highest and best use?

THE HERO'S JOURNEY

The world throws chaos, crisis, and commoditization at you. Chaos and crisis show up in obvious ways—it's just the world we live in. What is more insidious is the way the world attempts to commoditize everything and everyone. Including you, including us. To go along, to accept that what you do is just like what the next person does, and the next, and the next. That commoditization trap is the exact enemy you and we need to fight.

Too many people get stuck or never find the career success they are best designed for. They fail to find or reinforce or double down in their best leadership mode.

We introduced executive David Sheehan earlier in the book, and he sums up the arc of a career in operations roles in four phases. For him, first came GM, where he learned *what not to do*. Then he went to Toyota, a strong culture of hard-core manufacturing, sales, and distribution, where he learned *what to do*. Then he launched into project roles for a variety of companies, where he learned *how to do it*. The final and fourth stage he describes as *tying it all together*. Today he is completely energized by serving as a Fixer, drawing on his years of experience identifying and addressing what isn't working, then bringing organizations back to life.

Successful leaders look to their strengths as Fixers, Artists, Builders, or Strategists and fully embrace their distinct wiring and special superpowers. We all can tap into a different gear based on circumstances, but the best leaders are a dazzling demonstration of their deepest beliefs and continually improving capabilities.

Organizations are not off the hook here. We are all stakeholders in institutions where we can make our voices known and felt. In your work, you have a say about the quality of leadership within the organization and on your team even if you don't own the company. Most of us focus so much on being proactive in our health, wellness, and personal care. But what about our business health—are we taking the right approach to making sure we hire and promote the right leader for the right role?

PICK THE PERSON AND YOU PICK THE RESULT

Is leadership style predictive of success, or even more, is concentration within style predictive of success? We say yes.

If you want to sum up this book in one sentence, this is it: Pick the person and you pick the result.

- **Fixers** take on even the biggest crises. We are all vulnerable to global, national, and local effects of instability and disruptive change. Fixers work their magic to renew and strengthen teams, products, operations, processes, and communication. There is and will be no end of problems to solve.
- **Artists** take the necessary leap. That's vitally important, as exponential technologies challenge us at every turn, from AI, machine

learning and robotics to cryptocurrency, 3D printing, AR/VR, and gene editing. A spirit of rebellious innovation will continue to tackle static thinking and industries ripe for reinvention.

- **Builders** dominate markets, large or small. Competition can be intense and commoditizing in markets with many entrants or winner take all (like Google or Facebook), but with an expert Builder on board, organizations on the brink of explosive growth can experience breakthrough results with the right product, people, and process.

- **Strategists** move their organizations forward to be both dynamic and enduring. By 2020, half of the Fortune 500 listed in 2000 had died or been acquired. Superscalers keep the competitive edge, continuing to evolve and inspire their organizations even in the midst of a changing landscape, whether shifting culture, competition, or technological upheaval.

In your best FABS leadership mode, your genuine self and style is revealed in your outlook, mindset, actions, and results.

Set your compass before you venture out each day so that your demonstration of leadership both renews and strengthens your own sense of purpose and serves to advance your organization and everyone around you. Pick yourself and you pick your result.

Acknowledgments

First: our thanks to the brave executives who agreed to be interviewed. They had zero idea what we had in mind, and it's not like they were getting a call from, say, Malcolm Gladwell. No one was shown any questions in advance, just a request to get on a recorded call. And act natural. In most cases this wasn't a one and done. One conversation would lead to another conversation and then lots of follow-on advice from these brilliant leaders. And more than advice, we got such wonderful encouragement to press on, that we were on the right track. That helped us on our five-year journey in developing the FABS styles.

So: thank you, thank you, thank you to Cleve Adams, Rodney Armstead, Shan Atkins, Michelle Barnes, Michael Bartikoski, Joel Becker, Dr. John Behr, Carol Bernick, Richard Blain, Tom Britton, Griffin Caprio, Jeff Chalovich, Albert Chen, Andy Crestodina, Dr. Janine Davidson, Randy Deutsch, Jim Disanto, Jim Dolan, Michael Donner, Adrienne Duffy, Alex Eckelberry, Jaime Ellertson, Dan Epstein, Diana Fongheiser, Dave Freidman, Jeff Gordy, Daniel Hamburger, Justus Harris, Allen Hartley, Christie Hefner, Jayne Heggen, Troy Henikoff, Ken Hunt, David Johnson, Joshua Katz, Scott Keffer, Eric Kish, Matt Kunkel, Ryan Landry, Jeff Leitner, Bernie Liebowitz,

Richard Lindenmuth, Mike Lorelli, Jim Malackowski, Rudy Mazzocchi, Chris McAllister, Rob McClung, Jay Milligan, David Mitchelhill, Peter Murphy, Dr. Robert Murray, Jasmine Nahhas di Florio, Dave Ormesher, Leslie Pratch, Steve Raack, Russell Reeder, Bernie Rudnick, Rafael Salmi, Mhayse Samalya, Dean Samuels, Shawn Score, Susan Sentell, Marsha Serlin, Charlie Shalvoy, David Sheehan, John Short, Michael Sonnenfeldt, Patrick Spain, Verinder Syal, Glen Tullman, Siby Vadakekkara, Gaye van den Homberg, Whitney Vosburgh, John Wu, Lisa Yarnell, Mike Zawalski, and Barry Zekelman.

We want to thank the many incredible leaders, innovators, and problem solvers we have met over the years through our work at InterimExecs. You have been a continual source of inspiration for us and set the stage for observing FABS leadership styles in action. We thank our clients who let us see firsthand how bringing in the right leaders caused far-reaching improvement across your organizations and teams. It has been in seeing executives pave a better way forward that has confirmed for us what powerful leadership can accomplish.

This book was not possible but for the "yes" decision of our publishing team, starting with our agent, Dan Strutzel. Publisher Gilles Dana of G&D gave us the green light with his team, Evan Litzenblatt and Ellen Goldberg. Editor Sandra Wendel was our constant and good coach and whipped this book into much better shape. Especially after we'd lost all objectivity.

There is a special place in heaven for volunteers who agree to read someone else's manuscript. Our thanks to our beta readers Steve Vivian, Tom Underwood, Michael Tobin, Scott Keffer, Chris Killackey, Steve Hummel, Christine Matzen, Dan Foxx, and Catherine Rymsha.

Thanks to those who served as a sounding board for everything from cover design to the words weaved throughout the book: Ryan Henry, Zach Blum, Lauren Miller, Mike Davidson, Erin Davidson,

Abigail Pogrebin, Marc Boney, Jacob Friedman, Fern O'Neill, Meenakshi Dash, Michael Tobin, Lisa Jordan, Nikki Zollar, Shelley Frame, Jeffrey Jarmuth, Tommy Underwood, Bill Martens, Craig Landy, Paul Rosenbaum, John Moe, Jesse Frageman, Katie Hoffman, Sophie Jordan, Eliana Jordan, Shelley Frame, David Shapiro, Andy Wagner, Carol Wagner, Vicki Wolak, Jim Wolak, Jen Johnson, Tony Johnson, Lydia Johnson, Nolan Johnson, Jordan Friedman, Jacob Friedman, Andrew Friedman, and Craig Landy.

If we could write these acknowledgments in two parallel columns, there would be a second top list so we could properly thank our team for putting up with us on this project for year after year. Thank you for your invaluable contributions of smarts, ideas, and energy to Hannah Frageman, Paula Saban, Greg Voutsos, Cindy Richards, and FABS Leadership Assessment design expert Dr. Jeanne Hurlbert.

We wrote earlier in the book that none of us do it alone, and it applies to helping us think about and introduce us to leaders who best represent the FABS styles and principles we write about. Hats off to our friends Donna Zarcone and Barry Spencer for their help. And thank you to psychologist Dr. Robert Murray for his insights and sparks on leadership.

Our need to think deeply to figure out FABS leadership styles and develop a rigorous approach to developing the FABS Leadership Assessment, not to mention our company's InterimExecs RED Team, was advanced by leaps and bounds thanks to Robert's ongoing participation in the Strategic Coach program. Kudos to Dan Sullivan, Babs Smith, Adrienne Duffy, Maureen Sullivan and the crew at Strategic Coach for your brilliance and inspiration. You walk the talk like no other.

This book would not be possible without many late nights writing and editing, so thank you to our spouses—Brian Wagner and Sharon Jordan—for your love, support, and listening ear.

Index

About the Authors

It was 1995 and **Robert Jordan** was running *Online Access*, the first magazine to cover the internet. While at an industry conference, he had a chance run-in with a guy who handed him a business card that read "Interim CEO, Yahoo." This CEO—Philip Monego—had taken the Yahoo founders out of a trailer parked on campus at Stanford University, incorporated the company, created a board, and taken the company public. All in 180 days. It was this moment that changed Jordan's life.

After he sold *Online Access*, he dove into a new career working as an interim exec at tech companies, from working with Jeff Hawkins and Donna Dubinsky while marketing the breakout Palm Pilot to helping a big NASDAQ market maker launch a brand-new online trading platform. Along the path of launching and growing companies and helping other company founders, Jordan met hundreds of interim executives from around the world. In 2009 he launched a clubhouse for these like-minded executives, which then grew into Chicago-based InterimExecs, the premier matchmaker for smart organizations in need of expert leadership.

Jordan is the author of *How They Did It: Billion Dollar Insights from the Heart of America* and a Nightingale Conant audio program featuring interviews with champion company founders. He went to the University of Michigan and loves Ann Arbor. He is a lifelong Chicagoan, with a wife and two daughters plus two dogs. He spends his free time painting and creating mosaics with lots of color.

Olivia Wagner's leadership journey began at age seven when she started "Olivia's Mother's Helper Service" to score some cash while helping stay-at-home moms. Her empire grew: lemonade stands, car washes, inventing self-washing windshield wiper glasses, and craft sales, which led to lots of dreaming about what she would do when she grew up.

After her stint at the University of Michigan, she met Robert Jordan (another UM alum) and ventured to Chicago to start up a network for interim executives.

Wagner built the network from a homegrown website into a robust social network with thousands of members. She published an ebook, built a website and marking initiatives, and edited *How They Did It: Billion Dollar Insights from the Heart of America*. In conjunction with the book she led a national event series that drew hundreds of attendees. This ultimately led to cofounding InterimExecs with Jordan, which Wagner directs today with a mission to help companies get to a better future by matching them with the best leadership around the world.

Olivia Wagner is a Michigan native, recently making her return to the Detroit area with her husband and baby boy. She spends her free time outdoors, playing volleyball, seeking out farmers' markets (in the few nonwinter months in the heart of America) or cheering on University of Michigan.

CPSIA information can be obtained
at www.ICGtesting.com
Printed in the USA
JSHW031936170422
25019JS00001B/1